The U.S. Information Agency

The U.S. Information Agency

Clinton L. Doggett
and
Lois T. Doggett

CHELSEA HOUSE PUBLISHERS

On the cover: A Voice of America (VOA) broadcasting studio. The VOA's news and information programs reach most corners of the globe.
Frontispiece: In February 1986, to celebrate the 40th anniversary of USIA-sponsored broadcasting from West Berlin, a vintage U.S. Army truck used by RIAS-Radio in the 1940s drives around the city announcing the latest news.

Chelsea House Publishers
Editor-in-Chief: Nancy Toff
Executive Editor: Remmel T. Nunn
Managing Editor: Karyn Gullen Browne
Copy Chief: Juliann Barbato
Picture Editor: Adrian G. Allen
Art Director: Maria Epes
Manufacturing Manager: Gerald Levine

Know Your Government
Senior Editor: Kathy Kuhtz

Staff for THE U.S. INFORMATION AGENCY
Assistant Editor: James M. Cornelius
Deputy Copy Chief: Nicole Bowen
Editorial Assistant: Elizabeth Nix
Picture Coordinator: Melanie Sanford
Picture Researcher: Dixon & Turner Research Associates Inc.
Assistant Art Director: Loraine Machlin
Senior Designer: Noreen M. Lamb
Production Coordinator: Joseph Romano

First Printing

1 3 5 7 9 8 6 4 2

Library of Congress Cataloging-in-Publication Data
Doggett, Clinton L.
  U.S. Information Agency / Clinton L. Doggett, Lois T. Doggett.
    p.   cm.—(Know your government)
  Bibliography: p.
  Summary: Surveys the history of the U.S. Information Agency, describing its structure, function, and influence on American society.
  ISBN 1-55546-124-7.
      0-7910-0909-2 (pbk.)
1. United States Information Agency—History—Juvenile literature.
2. United States—Relations—Foreign countries—Juvenile literature.
[1. United States Information Agency. 2. United States—Relations—Foreign countries.] I. Doggett, Lois T. II. Title. III. Title: US Information Agency. IV. Title: United States Information Agency. V. Series: Know your government (New York, N.Y.)   88-742
E840.2.D64   1989   CIP
353.0089—dc19   AC

CONTENTS

KNOW YOUR GOVERNMENT

CHELSEA HOUSE PUBLISHERS

INTRODUCTION

Government: Crises of Confidence

Arthur M. Schlesinger, jr.

From the start, Americans have regarded their government with a mixture of reliance and mistrust. The men who founded the republic did not doubt the indispensability of government. "If men were angels," observed the 51st Federalist Paper, "no government would be necessary." But men are not angels. Because human beings are subject to wicked as well as to noble impulses, government was deemed essential to assure freedom and order.

At the same time, the American revolutionaries knew that government could also become a source of injury and oppression. The men who gathered in Philadelphia in 1787 to write the Constitution therefore had two purposes in mind. They wanted to establish a strong central authority and to limit that central authority's capacity to abuse its power.

To prevent the abuse of power, the Founding Fathers wrote two basic principles into the new Constitution. The principle of federalism divided power between the state governments and the central authority. The principle of the separation of powers subdivided the central authority itself into three branches—the executive, the legislative, and the judiciary—so that "each may be a check on the other." The *Know Your Government* series focuses on the major executive departments and agencies in these branches of the federal government.

The Constitution did not plan the executive branch in any detail. After vesting the executive power in the president, it assumed the existence of "executive departments" without specifying what these departments should be. Congress began defining their functions in 1789 by creating the Departments of State, Treasury, and War. The secretaries in charge of these departments made up President Washington's first cabinet. Congress also provided for a legal officer, and President Washington soon invited the attorney general, as he was called, to attend cabinet meetings. As need required, Congress created more executive departments.

Setting up the cabinet was only the first step in organizing the American state. With almost no guidance from the Constitution, President Washington, seconded by Alexander Hamilton, his brilliant secretary of the treasury, equipped the infant republic with a working administrative structure. The Federalists believed in both executive energy and executive accountability and set high standards for public appointments. The Jeffersonian opposition had less faith in strong government and preferred local government to the central authority. But when Jefferson himself became president in 1801, although he set out to change the direction of policy, he found no reason to alter the framework the Federalists had erected.

By 1801 there were about 3,000 federal civilian employees in a nation of a little more than 5 million people. Growth in territory and population steadily enlarged national responsibilities. Thirty years later, when Jackson was president, there were more than 11,000 government workers in a nation of 13 million. The federal establishment was increasing at a faster rate than the population.

Jackson's presidency brought significant changes in the federal service. He believed that the executive branch contained too many officials who saw their jobs as "species of property" and as "a means of promoting individual interest." Against the idea of a permanent service based on life tenure, Jackson argued for the periodic redistribution of federal offices, contending that this was the democratic way and that official duties could be made "so plain and simple that men of intelligence may readily qualify themselves for their performance." He called this policy rotation-in-office. His opponents called it the spoils system.

In fact, partisan legend exaggerated the extent of Jackson's removals. More than 80 percent of federal officeholders retained their jobs. Jackson discharged no larger a proportion of government workers than Jefferson had done a generation earlier. But the rise in these years of mass political parties gave federal patronage new importance as a means of building the party and of rewarding activists. Jackson's successors were less restrained in the distribu-

8

tion of spoils. As the federal establishment grew—to nearly 40,000 by 1861—the politicization of the public service excited increasing concern.

After the Civil War the spoils system became a major political issue. High-minded men condemned it as the root of all political evil. The spoilsmen, said the British commentator James Bryce, "have distorted and depraved the mechanism of politics." Patronage, by giving jobs to unqualified, incompetent, and dishonest persons, lowered the standards of public service and nourished corrupt political machines. Office-seekers pursued presidents and cabinet secretaries without mercy. "Patronage," said Ulysses S. Grant after his presidency, "is the bane of the presidential office." "Every time I appoint someone to office," said another political leader, "I make a hundred enemies and one ingrate." George William Curtis, the president of the National Civil Service Reform League, summed up the indictment. He said,

> The theory which perverts public trusts into party spoils, making public employment dependent upon personal favor and not on proved merit, necessarily ruins the self-respect of public employees, destroys the function of party in a republic, prostitutes elections into a desperate strife for personal profit, and degrades the national character by lowering the moral tone and standard of the country.

The object of civil service reform was to promote efficiency and honesty in the public service and to bring about the ethical regeneration of public life. Over bitter opposition from politicians, the reformers in 1883 passed the Pendleton Act, establishing a bipartisan Civil Service Commission, competitive examinations, and appointment on merit. The Pendleton Act also gave the president authority to extend by executive order the number of "classified" jobs—that is, jobs subject to the merit system. The act applied initially only to about 14,000 of the more than 100,000 federal positions. But by the end of the 19th century 40 percent of federal jobs had moved into the classified category.

Civil service reform was in part a response to the growing complexity of American life. As society grew more organized and problems more technical, official duties were no longer so plain and simple that any person of intelligence could perform them. In public service, as in other areas, the all-round man was yielding ground to the expert, the amateur to the professional. The excesses of the spoils system thus provoked the counter-ideal of scientific public administration, separate from politics and, as far as possible, insulated against it.

The cult of the expert, however, had its own excesses. The idea that administration could be divorced from policy was an illusion. And in the realm of policy, the expert, however much segregated from partisan politics, can never attain perfect objectivity. He remains the prisoner of his own set of values. It is these values rather than technical expertise that determine fundamental judgments of public policy. To turn over such judgments to experts, moreover, would be to abandon democracy itself; for in a democracy final decisions must be made by the people and their elected representatives. "The business of the expert," the British political scientist Harold Laski rightly said, "is to be on tap and not on top."

Politics, however, were deeply ingrained in American folkways. This meant intermittent tension between the presidential government, elected every four years by the people, and the permanent government, which saw presidents come and go while it went on forever. Sometimes the permanent government knew better than its political masters; sometimes it opposed or sabotaged valuable new initiatives. In the end a strong president with effective cabinet secretaries could make the permanent government responsive to presidential purpose, but it was often an exasperating struggle.

The struggle within the executive branch was less important, however, than the growing impatience with bureaucracy in society as a whole. The 20th century saw a considerable expansion of the federal establishment. The Great Depression and the New Deal led the national government to take on a variety of new responsibilities. The New Deal extended the federal regulatory apparatus. By 1940, in a nation of 130 million people, the number of federal workers for the first time passed the 1 million mark. The Second World War brought federal civilian employment to 3.8 million in 1945. With peace, the federal establishment declined to around 2 million by 1950. Then growth resumed, reaching 2.8 million by the 1980s.

The New Deal years saw rising criticism of "big government" and "bureaucracy." Businessmen resented federal regulation. Conservatives worried about the impact of paternalistic government on individual self-reliance, on community responsibility, and on economic and personal freedom. The nation in effect renewed the old debate between Hamilton and Jefferson in the early republic, although with an ironic exchange of positions. For the Hamiltonian constituency, the "rich and well-born," once the advocate of affirmative government, now condemned government intervention, while the Jeffersonian constituency, the plain people, once the advocate of a weak central government and of states' rights, now favored government intervention.

In the 1980s, with the presidency of Ronald Reagan, the debate has burst out with unusual intensity. According to conservatives, government intervention abridges liberty, stifles enterprise, and is inefficient, wasteful, and arbitrary. It disturbs the harmony of the self-adjusting market and creates worse troubles than it solves. Get government off our backs, according to the popular cliché, and our problems will solve themselves. When government is necessary, let it be at the local level, close to the people. Above all, stop the inexorable growth of the federal government.

In fact, for all the talk about the "swollen" and "bloated" bureaucracy, the federal establishment has not been growing as inexorably as many Americans seem to believe. In 1949, it consisted of 2.1 million people. Thirty years later, while the country had grown by 70 million, the federal force had grown only by 750,000. Federal workers were a smaller percentage of the population in 1985 than they were in 1955—or in 1940. The federal establishment, in short, has not kept pace with population growth. Moreover, national defense and the postal service account for 60 percent of federal employment.

Why then the widespread idea about the remorseless growth of government? It is partly because in the 1960s the national government assumed new and intrusive functions: affirmative action in civil rights, environmental protection, safety and health in the workplace, community organization, legal aid to the poor. Although this enlargement of the federal regulatory role was accompanied by marked growth in the size of government on all levels, the expansion has taken place primarily in state and local government. Whereas the federal force increased by only 27 percent in the 30 years after 1950, the state and local government force increased by an astonishing 212 percent.

Despite the statistics, the conviction flourishes in some minds that the national government is a steadily growing behemoth swallowing up the liberties of the people. The foes of Washington prefer local government, feeling it is closer to the people and therefore allegedly more responsive to popular needs. Obviously there is a great deal to be said for settling local questions locally. But local government is characteristically the government of the locally powerful. Historically, the way the locally powerless have won their human and constitutional rights has often been through appeal to the national government. The national government has vindicated racial justice against local bigotry, defended the Bill of Rights against local vigilantism, and protected natural resources against local greed. It has civilized industry and secured the rights of labor organizations. Had the states' rights creed prevailed, there would perhaps still be slavery in the United States.

The national authority, far from diminishing the individual, has given most Americans more personal dignity and liberty than ever before. The individual freedoms destroyed by the increase in national authority have been in the main the freedom to deny black Americans their rights as citizens; the freedom to put small children to work in mills and immigrants in sweatshops; the freedom to pay starvation wages, require barbarous working hours, and permit squalid working conditions; the freedom to deceive in the sale of goods and securities; the freedom to pollute the environment—all freedoms that, one supposes, a civilized nation can readily do without.

"Statements are made," said President John F. Kennedy in 1963, "labelling the Federal Government an outsider, an intruder, an adversary. . . . The United States Government is not a stranger or not an enemy. It is the people of fifty states joining in a national effort. . . . Only a great national effort by a great people working together can explore the mysteries of space, harvest the products at the bottom of the ocean, and mobilize the human, natural, and material resources of our lands."

So an old debate continues. However, Americans are of two minds. When pollsters ask large, spacious questions—Do you think government has become too involved in your lives? Do you think government should stop regulating business?—a sizable majority opposes big government. But when asked specific questions about the practical work of government—Do you favor social security? unemployment compensation? Medicare? health and safety standards in factories? environmental protection? government guarantee of jobs for everyone seeking employment? price and wage controls when inflation threatens?—a sizable majority approves of intervention.

In general, Americans do not want less government. What they want is more efficient government. They want government to do a better job. For a time in the 1970s, with Vietnam and Watergate, Americans lost confidence in the national government. In 1964, more than three-quarters of those polled had thought the national government could be trusted to do right most of the time. By 1980 only one-quarter was prepared to offer such trust. But by 1984 trust in the federal government to manage national affairs had climbed back to 45 percent.

Bureaucracy is a term of abuse. But it is impossible to run any large organization, whether public or private, without a bureaucracy's division of labor and hierarchy of authority. And we live in a world of large organizations. Without bureaucracy modern society would collapse. The problem is not to abolish bureaucracy, but to make it flexible, efficient, and capable of innovation.

Two hundred years after the drafting of the Constitution, Americans still regard government with a mixture of reliance and mistrust—a good combination. Mistrust is the best way to keep government reliable. Informed criticism

12

is the means of correcting governmental inefficiency, incompetence, and arbitrariness; that is, of best enabling government to play its essential role. For without government, we cannot attain the goals of the Founding Fathers. Without an understanding of government, we cannot have the informed criticism that makes government do the job right. It is the duty of every American citizen to know our government—which is what this series is all about.

J. William Fulbright (center) talks with a group of African scholars visiting the United States in 1986 under the aegis of the Fulbright Program. The former senator initiated the program in the 1940s; it is administered by the USIA.

ONE

Hands Across the Sea

Chances are that an American GI fighting against Japan in World War II would have listened once in a while to Tokyo Rose, broadcasting on shortwave radio. The GI would have heard a woman with a soft, pleasant voice and an American accent commiserating with him, commenting on his hardships and his homesickness, telling him that his commander in chief did not care how many American soldiers and sailors were killed. The object of the Tokyo Rose broadcasts was to demoralize American servicemen.

If a GI with the armed forces in Europe or North Africa had a shortwave radio, he might have heard Axis Sally broadcasting for the Nazis. She played "You'd Be So Nice to Come Home To" and other wistful wartime songs and asked him on the air if he thought his girlfriend was being true to him; the implication was that his girlfriend was not. In the weeks before D day, June 6, 1944, when the Allies invaded France on the Normandy coast, Axis Sally painted a vivid picture of the slaughter that would occur if the Allies ever dared dream of invading Adolf Hitler's stronghold. This is the kind of propaganda that American troops heard during the war.

The propaganda was not one-sided. The United States countered with radio broadcasts by the Voice of America (VOA), which, when it started in 1942, beamed programs from 36 transmitters in 25 languages. The VOA's approach

Iva Toguri D'Aquino (center), better known as Tokyo Rose, broadcast pro-Japanese propaganda in the Pacific region during World War II. Sentenced to 10 years in prison for treason, she is shown here upon her release in 1956.

was straightforward. It broadcast bad news as well as good, forthrightly explaining U.S. military and diplomatic policy during the war and defending U.S. actions.

The Voice of America was part of the Office of War Information (OWI), which operated an information service overseas. In 1946 the OWI became a branch of the Department of State, the diplomatic service of the federal government. The business of making and keeping friends abroad eventually became the responsibility of an independent entity, the United States Information Agency (USIA). Abroad, the USIA is known as the United States Information Service (USIS).

The Purpose of the USIA

The USIA is charged by Congress with the responsibility of managing the government's information, cultural, and educational exchange programs overseas. The agency is part of the executive branch of the government, so its director reports to the president. The director, his deputy, and four associate directors are appointed by the president and confirmed for their posts by the Senate.

The USIA's purpose and functions were originally outlined in the Fulbright Act of 1946, which provided for international, educational, and cultural exchange programs, and in the Smith-Mundt Act of 1948, which authorized information services overseas. The Fulbright-Hays Act of 1961 consolidated the 1946 Fulbright Act and other earlier legislation concerned with educational and cultural exchanges. Both the Smith-Mundt and the Fulbright-Hays acts describe the USIA's broad purpose as being to "increase mutual understanding between the people of the United States and the people of other countries."

The agency attempts to fulfill this mandate through a number of specific tasks. It seeks to promote understanding of American policies abroad, to win support for them, and to expose and refute foreign governments' distortions of American statements, which sometimes amount to counterpropaganda. The USIA analyzes reactions to U.S. policies in the foreign media and advises the president, the secretary of state, the National Security Council (an executive-branch agency that assesses U.S. defense needs and risks), and other high officials on the implications of foreign opinion. In a separate vein, the USIA helps articulate U.S. policy on the free flow of information worldwide. And in still another sphere, the agency administers educational and cultural exchange programs and participates in negotiations with foreign governments concerning these programs.

Despite their comparatively apolitical role, the cultural centers run by the USIS are not immune to danger. In 1989 a novel called *The Satanic Verses* by Salman Rushdie, who was born a Muslim in India, drew criticism from Muslim fundamentalists, who consider the book critical of their religion. When the book was published in the United States, a mob attacked the USIS center in Islamabad, Pakistan, breaking windows and burning the U.S. flag on the roof. The center had to close temporarily.

In all its tasks, the USIA works with private sector groups and individuals to improve the quality and extend the reach of its programs. The private sector has its say in USIA policy, too. The president appoints seven private citizens to serve on the U.S. Advisory Commission on Public Diplomacy, whose function is to ensure that the USIA is carrying out its tasks effectively and in a nonpartisan manner. That is, no program should bear the exclusive stamp of the Republican or Democratic party; rather, a broad range of American governmental and social ideals are to be conveyed. The commission reports each year to the president, the Congress, the secretary of state, and the USIA director.

A Muslim man carries a wounded comrade after police repulsed a mob attack on the USIS American Center in Islamabad, Pakistan, in February 1989. They were protesting the U.S. publication of The Satanic Verses, *a novel by Salman Rushdie that they considered insulting to their religion. The center was temporarily closed.*

18

The Modern Challenge

In this electronic age of instant communication, there are opinion molders all over the world. How does one put a human face on America's policies and actions? This task grows more demanding and challenging each year, and the USIA addresses it through a variety of programs, some simple and direct, others sophisticated and technologically advanced.

For instance, the USIA makes a videotape for international distribution of Dr. Michael DeBakey performing triple-bypass heart surgery. A USIA research officer appears on the "MacNeil/Lehrer NewsHour" on public television to discuss the way people in the Soviet Union perceive U.S. policies. A "footmobile" team from the USIS office in Kathmandu, Nepal, lugs movie equipment up a rocky Himalayan path to show films in an isolated village. An American basketball coach, working for USIA's Sports America program, runs a workshop for Somalia's national team. Yemeni citizens study English at the Yemeni-American Institute in their capital city, San'a. These are some of the ways in which the USIA has offered America's hand of friendship to people in other countries. Current and future programs will build upon what has worked, trying to put America in the best possible light without ignoring some of its shortcomings. American hands across the sea are not iron fists in velvet gloves; they are friendly overtures to seek acceptance of American views.

As every government's capacity to publicize itself expands, the world's people become more sensitive to the distinction between information and propaganda. If they perceive that foreign governments are trying to influence their opinions unduly, they may become suspicious of the message. The USIA is wary, then, that information can be used to mislead people. So it strives to use its ever-expanding communications apparatus—its hands across the sea—in new and beneficial ways.

In 1987, Andrew Young, former U.S. ambassador to the United Nations and then mayor of Atlanta, Georgia, speaks at the USIS Cultural Center in Harare, Zimbabwe, to mark the birthday of Dr. Martin Luther King, Jr. The USIA sponsored Young's trip.

TWO

Filling a Need

For a quarter century the USIA's mandate was strictly media-oriented: information only. Gradually the government came to recognize that hands across the sea could reinforce the voices through the air and the pictures on the screen, delivering the American message in a way that would enhance its effect many times over. Many members of Congress believed that person-to-person programs such as educational and cultural exchanges should be the responsibility of the agency in charge of information. Accordingly, the functions of the Bureau of Educational and Cultural Affairs in the Department of State were transferred to the USIA in 1978. The name of the expanded organization was changed to the United States International Communication Agency (USICA). In 1982, however, the agency's name was changed back to USIA, probably for good.

Sentiment was strong to retain the old name partly because the agency's organization and function had not changed. The USIA, as an independent agency that reports directly to the president, still takes its direction and policy guidance from the secretary of state in Washington and from U.S. ambassadors in the field.

The president appoints seven private citizens of both major political parties to the U.S. Advisory Commission on Public Diplomacy, whose function is to assess the USIA's policies and programs as well as other information, cultural, and educational exchange programs of the government. The members of the commission, drawn from academia and the business world, serve without pay. They meet with the director and other top officials of the USIA frequently, and from time to time with other people in and out of government to gauge current opinion in various fields, especially people whose jobs concern the news media, cultural affairs, and international communications.

How, Who, and Where

The USIA maintains a permanent presence in the capitals of 127 countries. In some of these countries, the USIS also has a post in other important cities or towns, for a total of 204 USIS posts worldwide. USIS officers in overseas posts report to an office in Washington, D.C., that serves a particular geographic area. The five area offices can draw upon all the expertise that headquarters offers to back up the field posts, providing technical and substantive help to the information and cultural programs they administer.

As of 1988, the USIA had authorized staff positions for 9,231 employees. Of these, 5,387 were Americans; the rest were people hired locally by the USIS offices. Only about 20 percent of the American staffers are assigned to overseas posts. Most are based in Washington or in other cities in the United States where VOA or Worldnet (the USIA's satellite television service) operate facilities.

The USIA Abroad

Because the USIA has diplomatic functions, its work is closely related to that of the Department of State, with which it is affiliated. In countries where the United States has an embassy, the USIS chief is the public affairs officer and also has the title of counselor of the embassy for public affairs. He or she is a member of what diplomats call the "country team." The country team advises the ambassador and is generally made up of local heads of government agencies represented at that post, such as the U.S. Agency for International Development, which runs U.S. economic aid in that country, and any U.S. military group with a presence there. The public affairs officer brings to the group his

Anthony C. E. Quinton (in dark jacket), U.S. ambassador to Kuwait, at a 1986 press conference; at far right is Public Affairs Officer Lee James Irwin of the USIA. The occasion was the 25th anniversary of U.S.-Kuwait relations; the meeting was widely covered in the local press.

or her expertise on public opinion both in the United States and abroad, as well as on matters having to do with education, cultural affairs, and the media.

In many countries, particularly the larger ones, the United States supplements its embassy in the capital city with a consulate in one or more other cities. In a consulate, foreign service officers handle visa matters and other limited diplomatic functions, and the USIS chief is designated the branch public affairs officer. In addition to this official, the USIS office may have American information and cultural affairs officers, who may in turn have American assistants. The information officer works with the media and is the mission's spokesperson to the local press. Either this officer or an assistant may be asked to provide help to American press, radio, and TV staff stationed in the country and to arrange press conferences for any American citizen there on an official visit.

The cultural affairs officer is in charge of educational and cultural programs. He or she serves on the board of the exchange commission that oversees the Fulbright Program if there is one in the country or, if there is not, directly manages the United States educational exchange programs.

At a small post where the public affairs officer may be the only American official, he or she will perform the duties of information and cultural affairs officers as well as those of the public affairs officer. In all posts, large and small, local people are employed to assist in administrative positions and in the USIA's programs.

The USIA at Home

In Washington, D.C., the USIA's functions are of two kinds. One, it supports the work done overseas. Two, it gives feedback to the U.S. government from its missions abroad and from foreign news sources.

The five area offices back up the field offices with all kinds of services: They propose candidates for positions in the USIS offices; allocate funds for the work in the field; obtain materials for information, education, and cultural programs;

The Voice of America newsroom in Washington, D.C. About 80 percent of the USIA's 9,200 employees work in the United States, mainly in information services such as radio broadcasting and news dissemination.

and provide speakers, videotapes, exhibits, and so forth. Computers link them with most of the posts overseas. Thus the libraries and information centers all over the world can tap into data bases in Washington or elsewhere in the network, gaining access to up-to-date and official information on U.S. policies and actions. Similarly, the headquarters has instant access to information and analysis from the field on matters of concern to decision makers.

Sometimes an item in the news reflects badly on the image of America that the agency wants to present to the world. Stories about drug abuse, for instance, or about racial incidents are not flattering. Staff members in Washington are prepared to offer guidance on damage control—not covering up, not suppressing a story, but suggesting ways to present it in the best possible light: refuting erroneous or malicious reports, presenting details that might help to justify an action, or pointing out some favorable elements in an otherwise negative story.

As a means of countering adverse propaganda on American attitudes and actions, the USIA is prompt to expose and refute attempts at disinformation in the foreign media. (Disinformation is any type of falsity spread in order to influence public opinion.) For example, a story planted in the Nigerian press in the early 1980s indicated that the United States was at work on a weapon that would kill blacks but not whites. USIS officers abroad, as well as the government in Washington, have access to the USIA's monthly publication *Soviet Propaganda Alert*.

The USIA also operates a service called "Dateline America," which transmits worldwide news items and feature stories that emphasize positive elements on the American scene—the latest advances in space technology, for example, or news about the Special Olympics for handicapped children. As standard guidance, the USIA continually updates a set of guidelines called "worldwide priority themes." These outline the kinds of stories that make America look good. The strengths of the economy, social programs, progress toward racial equality, scientific achievements, private enterprise, and international cooperation are some of the themes that the media can emphasize in their presentations. Besides these stateside topics, the USIA offers guidance to its missions on how to treat subjects of local concern: what position to take, for instance on the subject of the unification of North and South in Korea or the East and West in Berlin.

The functions of the agency that relate to its feedback role are similarly diverse. The USIA briefs and advises the president, the National Security Council, the Department of State, and other agencies of government concerned with foreign affairs. The director of the USIA attends meetings of the National

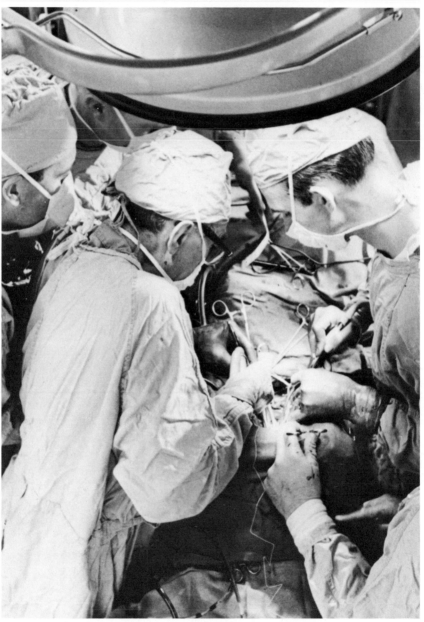

Dr. Michael DeBakey (center) performs heart surgery in 1965. The USIA videotaped this operation for international distribution as part of the effort to publicize advances in medicine and in other aspects of American life.

Security Council and is invited to attend cabinet meetings when the agenda concerns the agency's work. In a daily bulletin distributed to the executive branch of the government and to members of Congress, USIA staff summarize the reactions in the foreign media to American policies and actions. Every day the secretary of state holds a policy meeting attended by the director or deputy director of the USIA, who is able to provide analyses of comments in the foreign press on issues of the day. In this way, the USIA participates directly in the formulation of American policy.

It is not part of the USIA's mandate to deal with the media in the United States. That responsibility rests with the Bureau of Public Affairs in the Department of State. The USIA does not disseminate within the United States the materials it prepares; they are for overseas use only. (Congress forbids domestic distribution, fearing that the government could use the USIA for propaganda at home as was done in Nazi Germany and is still done in many nations.) However, these materials are made available at its Washington headquarters, after being released abroad, for the benefit of members of Congress, researchers, and the American media. The USIA's Office of Research puts out reports on views expressed in foreign media, which are available at 30 university libraries and institutions throughout the country.

Hand in Hand with the Private Sector

The USIA's total budget for fiscal year 1988 was $820 million. However, the agency can also look to the private sector for contributions of expertise, services, and materials; the private sector might also finance programs or parts of programs. Indeed, involvement of people who are not in government is much more than just an economic measure: It is an integral part of the agency's policy to present to the world a true picture of the whole of American life. For this reason the USIA welcomes the involvement of public-spirited private citizens in its efforts, and the agency profits from the counsel of advisory committees made up of people in business, academia, the entertainment profession, and other walks of life.

Nonprofit institutions, both American and foreign, cooperate with the USIA in many types of projects. The agency can call, for instance, on the Red Cross, 4-H clubs, church groups, or the League of Women Voters to advise and assist in exchange programs and other USIA programs. Thus with its limited budget the USIA can make its resources go further. More important, its programs reflect the genuine concerns of people in the States who support efforts to explain American culture to people abroad.

President Richard Nixon (third from right) meets with USIA Director Frank Shakespeare (on Nixon's right) and members of the U.S. Advisory Commission on Public Diplomacy in the White House in 1971 to get a perspective from the private sector. USIA officials confer frequently with top government figures.

For expos and trade fairs American manufacturers sometimes lend or donate products to be exhibited by the USIA. They may also support the exhibits in various other ways, such as providing personnel, transportation, construction help, training for fair workers, or direct financial support.

Leaders in the private sector participate in five committees that advise on libraries, radio broadcasting, radio engineering, television, and medicine. There are in addition five other advisory groups of private citizens who are authorities in the fields of sports, public relations, labor, TV and films, and marketing. More than 200 volunteers, whose services are valued at $100 million, contribute their time and expertise to these functions.

Another private sector advisory group is the International Council, a group of nearly 100 American and foreign business leaders created by the USIA in 1987 to assess the views held in other countries on American foreign policy. The council held its second meeting in June 1988. Prominent among the issues discussed were relations with the Soviet Union, the Iran-Iraq War, the United

States budget deficit, trade policy, aid to the contras in Nicaragua, deteriorating relations with Panama over charges that its government is dealing in drugs, military and economic aid to poor countries, drug trafficking elsewhere, and Third World debt. The council constitutes a valuable sounding board of how American and foreign leaders of public opinion react to the U.S. government's policies and actions.

Benjamin Franklin (left) in the palace of Versailles in 1778. Franklin, who could be called the first American information officer, was well received in the courts of Europe as the new nation tried to win diplomatic recognition during the revolutionary war.

THREE

Striped Pants, Khaki, and Shirtsleeves

Information has been an instrument of American foreign policy since the beginning of the nation's history. Even during the American Revolution the Continental Congress sent envoys to establish ties with European leaders. One of these was Benjamin Franklin, who represented the American colonies in Paris. According to one anecdote, he supposedly remarked that the duty of an ambassador was to lie abroad for his country. (An obsolete meaning of "lying abroad" is staying away from home for some time.) Levity aside, Franklin performed some of the duties of a present-day information officer. One of his tasks in Paris was to try to convince the French that it was in their interest to help the American colonies achieve independence from Great Britain. He wrote articles for French newspapers that championed the principles of the American Revolution, and he sent reports back to his government on the French leaders' current opinions. He became a darling of French society, performing the duties of a cultural affairs officer, one might say, in attending salons, concerts, and art shows.

Precursors of the USIA

Franklin, however, was an exception. During America's first century of independent existence, ambassadors acted more ambassadorial: Diplomatic exchanges were conducted strictly between one government and another. The profession of diplomacy was dignified and solemn; indeed, many of the early American presidents served overseas before attaining the White House. (George Bush, a former ambassador to China, is one of only three presidents since the Civil War with overseas experience.) By the late 1800s, elegant striped pants were the favored garb of the diplomatic corps.

Meanwhile, the American people were consumed with the huge task of building their new nation, and there was neither the time nor the need to engage in cultural and information exchanges with other countries. The burden of domestic problems was one reason for this focus. Another reason was spelled out more clearly in the Monroe Doctrine, named for President James Monroe (1817–25) and defined by him in 1823. The doctrine expressed, among other things, America's wish to steer clear of foreign entanglements, especially wars and peacetime alliances with European powers. This isolationist sentiment sprang from the belief that European nations had often been dragged into wars to fulfill an alliance or out of a sense of honor rather than national interest. The young United States did not want to make the same mistake, and managed to abide by the doctrine until 1917, when it entered World War I.

In fact, the times prevented close contact with potential allies overseas. Wide oceans both east and west of the continent, arduous travel conditions, and undeveloped means of communication all served to discourage efforts to maintain relations with foreign people or governments. Not until World War II did the U.S. government pay attention to international exchanges in peacetime; only war called attention to the necessity of regular contact.

The first real precursor of the USIA was the Creel Committee, or the Committee on Public Information, which President Woodrow Wilson established during World War I in order to administer propaganda activities both at home and abroad. Its head, George Creel, believed that the nation, to safeguard military secrets, could rely on voluntary cooperation by the press rather than on censorship. (Nonetheless, the Espionage Act of 1917 did decree harsh penalties for anyone who wrote anything critical of the war effort or that eroded the morale of the troops.) Creel applied his managerial talents to building a dynamic organization that enlisted support for the war at home and conducted propaganda activities abroad. As soon as the war was over, the Creel Committee's work was terminated.

In 1917, George Creel, a former journalist, was named to head the Committee on Public Information, a precursor of the USIA. Part of the war effort for World War I, the committee was meant to supplement the formal diplomatic process by providing a variety of information to the public.

In contrast to the insular attitude of the American government, the leadership in Russia, Italy, and Germany made extensive use of propaganda techniques in the years between the two world wars. At first, governments directed their efforts at their own citizens; later they addressed an international audience. In the popular American view, the word "propaganda" came to have a disreputable connotation and the practice of it was considered beneath the dignity of decent Americans.

Only in 1938, when propaganda from the Fascist governments of Germany and Italy began to permeate Latin America, did President Franklin D. Roosevelt recognize the need for countermeasures. The U.S. government finally entered the field of international cultural exchanges with the creation of an Interdepartmental Committee for Scientific Cooperation and, in the Department of State, a Division of Cultural Cooperation. Notwithstanding their lofty titles, in which the word "information" was not even mentioned, these bodies had the task of combating anti-American propaganda under the aegis of Roosevelt's Good Neighbor Policy. (Under the policy, the United States vowed to cease interfering in Latin American affairs.) Two or three other committees

Actors rehearse a radio show, "You Can't Do Business with Hitler," produced by the Office of War Information (OWI). The USIA, successor to the OWI, was created in part to counteract enemy propaganda during World War II, but with a vital difference: Whenever possible, the USIA's output would be based on facts.

with equally high-sounding names directed their attention to relations with Latin America. When in 1941 American involvement in World War II began to seem inevitable, the government set up machinery to gather intelligence and disseminate information abroad and to elicit support for the defense effort at home. Many of the information specialists were now arrayed not in striped pants but in the military's olive drab.

During the war the United States recognized that it had to undertake a serious overseas propaganda campaign, but the American information service would not imitate the distortions and falsehoods of enemy propaganda. In 1942 the Voice of America started broadcasting, and from the beginning this radio service was dedicated to factual reporting. In its first program the announcer said, "The news may be good or bad. We shall tell you the truth." Before and during the war several other bureaus were created to tackle matters of public information, intelligence gathering, trade relations, and cultural diplomacy. These bureaus included the Coordinator of Information, the Office of Emergency Management, and the Coordinator of Inter-American Affairs, to name only a few. Understandably, the plethora of agencies created some confusion, which was largely resolved when most of them were brought under the umbrella of the Office of War Information (OWI).

General Dwight D. Eisenhower, who commanded the Allied forces in Europe for the last two years of the war, gave the OWI considerable credit. After the war was over he said, "The expenditure of men and money in wielding the spoken and written word was an important contributing factor in undermining the enemy's will to resist and supporting the fighting morale of our potential allies." Nevertheless, when the boys came home, the American public was tired of the war and everything to do with it. Wartime agencies, including the OWI, shut down, but the Voice of America continued.

The Cold War Heats Up

Relations between the United States and the Soviet Union worsened dramatically after the war. The two powers were no longer allied in the common cause

The Nazis dropped these cartoon leaflets over Italy in 1944 in an effort to depress morale among U.S. troops. When the cold war began the next year, the Soviet Union launched a similar propaganda drive to diminish the world's opinion of America.

of defeating the Nazi menace; the spread of Soviet influence now alarmed the free world. So it was that information activities, conducted now by shirtsleeved men behind the scenes, took on the role of instruments of confrontation between opposing ideologies. Often, ideological conflict stopped just inches or hours short of open hostility. In the cold war, as this war of words and ideas came to be known, some old terms took on new meanings for the modern context, including *imperialism* and *hegemony*—both sides accused the other not of military imperialism but of political and ideological coercion. And certain new buzz words that had considerable force in shaping public opinion and official actions also arose: *iron curtain, containment, détente.*

The first of these new terms was coined by Winston Churchill, wartime prime minister of Great Britain, who said in 1946, "from Stettin in the Baltic to Trieste in the Adriatic, an iron curtain has descended across the Continent." In the decade after 1945, as the Soviet Union imposed its rule on the countries of Eastern Europe, this concept helped to shape the foreign policy of the United States. The policy came to be known as containment as described and recommended by George F. Kennan, the foremost expert of the day on Soviet affairs. Kennan suggested in 1947 "a long-term, patient but firm and vigilant containment of Russia's expansive tendencies." The concept was embodied in the Truman Doctrine, spelled out by President Harry S. Truman in 1947 in a speech to Congress in which he avowed that the United States was determined to help "free peoples" resist "attempted subjugation by armed minorities or by outside pressures."

President Truman did not want the United States to compete aggressively with the propaganda activities of other countries, but he did want to make sure "that other people receive a full and fair picture of American life and of the aims and policies of the United States."

The cold war intensified perilously in 1948–49, when the USSR tried to impose a blockade around those sectors of Berlin administered by the Allies. With all surface transport cut off, the beleaguered city was sustained by provisions that arrived in a massive airlift lasting 11 months, which delivered more than 2 million tons of supplies and ferried out Berlin's industrial exports.

The North Atlantic Treaty Organization (NATO) was formed in 1949 to counter the military buildup of Communist forces in Eastern Europe. Most of the countries of Western Europe, plus the United States and Canada, signed the treaty. The member nations committed themselves to come to the aid of any one of their number that suffered an armed attack. With this commitment, the United States dropped forever its residual faith in the isolationism as

Twenty tons of flour arrive by U.S. Air Force transport in Berlin, Germany, in 1948, after the Soviets blocked the roads to the city. The Berlin airlift was an early success in the U.S. effort to win world favor during the cold war.

defined by the Monroe Doctrine. America would now participate in a broad alliance bent on protecting and advancing the interests of the West.

On the other side of the world, the Soviets supported the Communist government of North Korea when it attacked South Korea in 1950. The United Nations went to the defense of South Korea, with the United States providing most of the men and material for the so-called police action. The non-Communist participants in this conflict, which lasted until 1953, failed to achieve their purpose of unifying the Korean peninsula into a single democratic state, but they succeeded in giving notice to the aggressors that the United States and the rest of the free world would not tolerate encroachment on their territories by Communist-controlled belligerents.

The chill produced by the cold war, which dominated foreign relations during the Truman administration, also had a glacial effect on domestic affairs at the turn of the decade. During the campaign for the congressional elections of 1950, the Republicans accused the Democratic administration of being "soft on Communism." Senator Joseph McCarthy of Wisconsin exploited widespread fears that the government was infiltrated by Communist spies. He made unsubstantiated claims that many Communists and fellow travelers were on the payroll of the Department of State. In 1950 President Truman, responding to the anticommunist sentiments of the American people, initiated a "Campaign of Truth" to counter Communist propaganda. Congress voted lavish funds for this purpose.

During the first year or two of the 1950s, the impact of the McCarthy witch-hunt badly weakened the staffs engaged in foreign policy and information services. In disarray and nearly paralyzed, these bureaus replaced their balanced and objective offerings with strident, aggressive anticommunist outpourings.

Against the backdrop of these belligerent moves, the government was taking peaceful steps to promote American values and to counter the hostility of those who did not share its views. In 1946 Congress passed the Fulbright Act, creating the educational exchange program that aimed to increase mutual understanding between Americans and people of other countries. (See the section on exchanges in Chapter Seven.) By means of the Smith-Mundt Act (1948), Congress established the information program as an official element of diplomacy.

President Harry Truman speaks to the first representatives to the North Atlantic Treaty Organization (NATO), in Washington, D.C., 1949. USIA officers frequently solicit opinions from NATO leaders as a way of gauging public sentiment in allied nations.

Senator Joseph McCarthy (left) interrupts the proceedings of a Senate investigatory committee in 1954. McCarthy claimed that Communists had infiltrated the federal government. Though his investigation was later discredited, hundreds of USIA and State Department employees lost their jobs or were blacklisted, and morale suffered for years.

When Dwight D. Eisenhower became president in 1953, he commissioned studies on ways to strengthen the information service. On the basis of the studies, he decided to create an agency independent of the Department of State. His decision was endorsed by his secretary of state, John Foster Dulles, who preferred to concentrate on policy and leave the management of programs to others; Dulles would retain responsibility for policy guidance in information matters. Eisenhower's decision was the genesis of the USIA, which immediately found itself on the ideological front lines.

Customers line up in Moscow to buy America Illustrated, *a monthly magazine published in Russian by the USIA. The agency tries to furnish people abroad with accurate information about life in the United States in order to combat the disinformation circulated by unfriendly governments.*

FOUR

Information in the
Space Age

When the USIA was established in 1953, its mission, as stated in a presidential directive, was "to submit evidence to peoples of other nations by means of communication techniques that the objectives and policies of the United States are in harmony with and will advance their legitimate aspirations for freedom, progress, and peace." The new agency's mandate did not include educational and cultural exchange programs; until 1978 these were administered by a division of the Department of State.

President Eisenhower appointed the first director of the USIA, Theodore Streibert, on the strength of his reputation as an effective manager in radio broadcasting. Streibert set up the organization like a business, with assistant directors acting as vice-presidents in charge of USIA activities in specific geographic areas.

Eisenhower viewed information services as vital to national security, but the newly independent agency entrusted with these tasks did not enjoy the support it needed to carry them out effectively. McCarthyism was still a strong influence on foreign and domestic policy in these years, and the Communist party was outlawed. Government employees who were judged to be security risks were fired. Morale was low, particularly in the Department of State and the USIA, where McCarthy's ax had fallen heavily. The agency was demoralized and hobbled by budget cuts.

A turn came in 1955 when the Warsaw Pact was signed. The pact unified the military machines of eight Eastern European countries: Albania (which withdrew in 1961), Bulgaria, Czechoslovakia, East Germany, Hungary, Poland, Romania, and the Soviet Union. To face this new military threat, NATO bolstered its forces. Meanwhile, the U.S. government mounted the People-to-People program, a means of getting private organizations to work with their counterparts abroad. With this effort Eisenhower hoped to win support in the international community for his Atoms for Peace plan for diverting nuclear

President Dwight D. Eisenhower presents his Atoms for Peace plan to the United Nations in 1953, proposing to redirect American work on nuclear power away from military and toward scientific ends. Eisenhower was among the first to consider such appeals to world opinion vital to national security.

Rioters wrecked the U.S. embassy and this room in the USIS Center in Taipei, Taiwan, in 1957. Hostility toward America's support of Chinese Nationalists in their struggle against Communists brought the agency and its activities under attack.

science from war to the pursuit of human welfare. He gave the USIA oversight of this program as well.

Marxist regimes in many parts of the world enjoyed growing prestige in these years. They owed their ascent partly to diplomatic and military successes and partly to their effective information programs. In many parts of the world propagandists had succeeded in stirring up anti-American passions. USIS libraries, highly visible and vulnerable targets, sometimes suffered attacks from rioters who smashed equipment and burned books. Animosity was especially rife in Asia, where the United States supported the Nationalist Chinese regime in Taiwan against the mainland Chinese, and in Latin America, where U.S. activity was perceived as interference in domestic affairs. Circumstances at home and abroad presented the USIA with several challenges: how to help America regain the good opinion and goodwill of people overseas, how to convey America's desire not to engage in nuclear war—in short, how to carry out its mission as described at the start of this chapter.

In the late 1950s the USIA was striving to reach audiences worldwide in many languages by various means: radio, news publications, bookmobiles, mobile film units, even television. A proven method of inspiring goodwill was to extend the hand of friendship to people at fairs and exhibitions. An early opportunity to do this came in 1954 when, with the cooperation of private industry, the USIA exhibited a film industry innovation called "This Is Cinerama" at a trade fair in Damascus, Syria. (The Cinerama process allows film to be shown in a complete circle around the audience.) The show was very popular, and its success was such that the Soviets, whose entry did not draw large crowds, claimed that Cinerama was actually a Russian invention and the American exhibit only an imitation. Nevertheless, when the Cinerama film was to be shown at a fair in Bangkok, Thailand, the Soviets withdrew their exhibit rather than compete again with the USIA's show.

Information Pierces the Iron Curtain

George V. Allen became USIA director in 1957. He had been director once before, in 1948–49, when the information service was still part of the Department of State. Between these jobs he had had a distinguished career as a diplomat, so he appreciated the importance of information as a diplomatic tool. In his opinion the agency should not merely react to the news of the day, but should take a longer view. Under his leadership the USIA began to have a greater role in the formulation of foreign policy. He set high standards of objectivity and balanced presentation of issues.

An important target of information programs has been the large and varied population of the Soviet Union. Before 1955 the Soviets censored all American printed material that was allowed into their country, but toward the end of that year the two nations agreed that a USIA magazine, *America Illustrated*, which presents factual material on life in the United States, could be distributed in the USSR without being censored. So in 1956 the first 50,000 copies of the Russian-language issue of the magazine went on sale in the USSR. To reciprocate, the United States agreed to allow the Soviets to distribute their magazine, *USSR*, in America.

The USIA penetrated the iron curtain further in 1959 with an entry at the American National Exhibition in Moscow. There, 75 Russian-speaking guides trained by the USIA attended to the fair goers, while a robot named Ramac (really an electronic brain) responded in Russian to questions about the United States. A film produced by Walt Disney, *Circarama*, and a photograph

44

One of the displays at the American National Exhibition in Moscow in 1959. The show also included the screening of a film innovation called Circarama (produced by Walt Disney) and a demonstration of a prototype robot.

collection entitled "Family of Man," seen earlier at the Museum of Modern Art in New York City, both drew large crowds.

That same year Soviet premier Nikita Khrushchev visited the United States to meet with President Eisenhower at Camp David, the president's weekend retreat in rural Maryland. With this opportunity to improve relations, the Soviets stopped jamming Voice of America broadcasts during the summit meeting. But the warming quickly cooled in May 1960 when a Soviet fighter plane shot down an American spy plane over Soviet territory. The downing, known as the U-2 incident, marked the end of the rapprochement, or harmonious relations. The Soviets withdrew their invitation to President Eisenhower to return Khrushchev's visit, and they resumed jamming VOA broadcasts.

Glory and Grief

When John F. Kennedy took office as president in 1961, he delivered an inaugural address that sounded a new tone for American society. He called for the nation to unite in the struggle against tyranny, poverty, disease, and war.

A section of the Berlin Wall, built in 1961. Relations between the U.S. and the USSR worsened when the Soviets built the wall to keep people from leaving Communist East Berlin for the West.

Although Kennedy insisted that he sought a peaceful solution to superpower frictions in Germany, the United States beefed up its military presence in Europe. Shortly thereafter, the two powers came into conflict over the status of Berlin, which had been divided into four zones of occupation since World War II—one each for France, Great Britain, the United States, and the USSR. Premier Khrushchev hinted at military action to settle the issue on his terms. About 200,000 East German refugees streamed into the western zones, and the East German government started to build the Berlin Wall, which still physically divides the city. When President Kennedy visited Berlin he addressed a cheering crowd, telling them, "Ich bin auch ein Berliner," ("I too am a Berliner"), reassuring them of America's moral and political support for the freedom of the city.

He did not cover himself with glory, however, when in April 1961 he secretly authorized 1,200 Cuban exiles living in America to invade their native island. The assault, supported with U.S. supplies and funds, was intended to overthrow the regime of Fidel Castro, who had come to power in 1959. It failed—largely because of faulty information fed to Kennedy's staff about the attacking force's capabilities and the strength of Castro's defense. This fiasco at the small Cuban port called the Bay of Pigs was a different kind of challenge for the information services, which were obliged to make the best of a deeply embarrassing situation. On the positive side, one of Kennedy's first moves as president was to launch the Alliance for Progress, a 10-year plan aimed at raising living standards in Latin America with U.S. support. The USIA did much to publicize the plan.

By October 1962 the Soviets, possibly fearing another invasion by U.S.-backed forces, had installed in Cuba ballistic missiles capable of hitting targets in the United States. President Kennedy ordered a naval blockade to prevent the delivery of additional missiles to Cuba. The Soviets backed down. They quickly agreed to dismantle the missile base.

This incident, known as the Cuban missile crisis, inflamed world opinion. Attention focused on the threat of a holocaust if nuclear arms continued to be developed by the superpowers or any other countries capable of producing these weapons. In 1963 three nations—the United States, the United Kingdom, and the USSR—signed a treaty outlawing tests of nuclear armaments in the atmosphere, in space, and under water. Within months more than 100 other countries agreed to the treaty. In fact, the treaty has no teeth: It does not forbid underground testing, the signatories do not agree to cease stockpiling weapons already developed, and there are no provisions for international supervision.

The task for the information services in such a climate is daunting. They have the unpleasant responsibility for keeping the nuclear threat always in the public consciousness, in the hope that potential malefactors will be deterred by the force of the world's condemnation of nuclear warfare.

In 1963 President Kennedy signed a statement that redefined the mission of the United States Information Agency. The agency would not merely "submit evidence" that American policies were in harmony with the aspirations of people in other countries, as the Eisenhower statement had said. Rather, the USIA was to do much more: "to influence public attitudes," promote support abroad for the freedom of people to choose their own governments, emphasize American leadership, and expose attempts at disinformation on the part of other governments. The new approach was more activist, requiring that information and propaganda efforts be taken directly to the world.

President Kennedy appointed Edward R. Murrow director of the USIA in 1961. Murrow had been a popular figure in radio broadcasting during and after World War II. On his weekly program "Hear It Now," his electrifying descriptions of the German occupation of Austria, the Battle of Britain, and

47

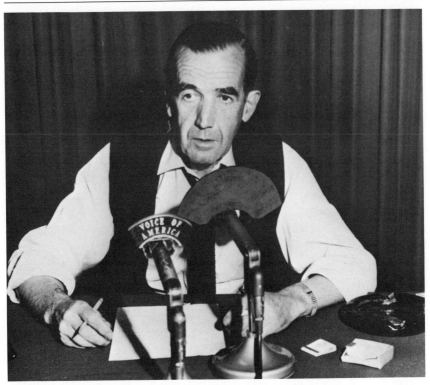

Veteran broadcaster Edward R. Murrow was named USIA director in 1963. He gave added prestige to USIA operations by insisting on accuracy, by focusing on foreign policy, and by working closely with the White House.

other momentous events kept radio audiences enrapt. With the advent of television, his "See It Now" likewise became a model of forceful, truthful news reporting.

As USIA director, Murrow was determined to overcome the disadvantages of scattershot programming, especially because budgetary restrictions precluded wide distribution of the message. He insisted on targeting specific audiences and using the most effective techniques to drive the message home. Furthermore, he insisted on accuracy and credibility in all the agency's products. He established a closer dialogue with the White House and concentrated on foreign policy issues in USIA programs.

When President Kennedy was assassinated in November 1963, the USIA had the sorrowful duty of informing the world about the tragedy. It then quickly produced a film on the presidency in 39 languages and distributed it to 111 countries. A year later the USIA released for even wider distribution a full-length documentary on the JFK administration: *John F. Kennedy: Years of Lightning, Day of Drums*.

Vietnam and After

During the 1960s the VOA's programmers enhanced the appeal of transmissions by emphasizing American pop culture: jazz, slangy dialogue, and comedy skits as well as more serious programs. Every week VOA's audience, according to USIA estimates, was more than 40 million listeners.

In one area, the work was not so lighthearted. The USIA was trying to help the government of South Vietnam improve its equipment and techniques for countering propaganda from North Vietnam and from the Vietcong, the pro-Communist guerrilla forces operating in the South. The agency also assisted in the pacification program that tried to win the support of the civilian population for the government's policies and military actions. One element of the psychological warfare was to drop leaflets on North Vietnam and the areas of South Vietnam controlled by the Vietcong. Designed to weaken the Communists' support, the leaflets also warned the people to avoid those areas targeted by bombers from the South. Separately, the agency helped in the amnesty program, whereby former Communist sympathizers were forgiven once they switched sides; and in the indoctrination of refugees, whereby people fleeing the North were taught the American point of view.

Throughout the administration of President Lyndon Johnson, the United States stepped up its military attack on pro-Communist Vietnamese. The most palpable moves were such widely condemned actions as bombing North Vietnam and spraying massive amounts of jungle defoliants (chemical dust that makes leaves fall off prematurely), especially Agent Orange, which some people think caused cancer and other illnesses in U.S. servicemen exposed to it. The USIA had the difficult task of presenting these actions in a favorable light while giving away nothing about American attempts to achieve a negotiated peace. The agency distributed a documentary film about Vietnam, *Night of the Dragon*. It was dubbed in 23 languages and shown on TV and in theaters in 110 countries. Reporting on life in America, the USIA depicted the violent antiwar protests on college campuses and elsewhere in the country.

More peaceful and productive was the USIA's role in a campaign in Laos, Vietnam's western neighbor, to increase rice production. In 1967 the USIS office in the Laotian capital of Vientiane ran a contest for amateur bands and

Two U.S. Air Force planes spray the liquid defoliant Agent Orange over en-emy territory in 1966, during the Vietnam War. Besides broadcasting positive news, the USIA must also inform the world of unpopular U.S. actions.

songwriters to come up with a commercial that urged farmers to plant rice and promised help from the government. The winning jingle was broadcast on the radio.

Meanwhile, at Expo 67 in Montreal, Quebec, the U.S. exhibit, produced by the USIA, attracted more than 5 million visitors. One of the main features was the building in which the exhibit was housed, a geodesic dome created by the American architect R. Buckminster Fuller.

The U.S. Pavilion at Expo 67 in Montreal, Quebec, was housed in a geodesic dome designed by architect R. Buckminster Fuller. The USIA is responsible for mounting the U.S. exhibit at such fairs, striving to incorporate the latest technology.

From top: *Astronauts Neil Armstrong, Buzz Aldrin, and Michael Collins, with a full-scale model of the* Apollo 11 *craft they rode to the moon. The USIA built the model and organized the astronauts' stop in Bombay, India, in 1970.*

Détente

In his first term as president (1969–73), Richard Nixon modified the policy guidance given to the USIA. Nixon and Secretary of State Henry Kissinger shifted the emphasis of foreign policy toward détente, the easing of tensions with the Soviets. The shift stemmed in part from both countries' preoccupation with matters other than ideological confrontation. Americans were exerting pressure on the White House to get out of Vietnam and to reduce foreign commitments in general. The Kremlin was beset by economic problems and growing conflict with China. Nixon issued a call for negotiation to replace confrontation. He succeeded to the extent that the Soviets were persuaded to enter into talks on the reduction of military forces in Europe.

In 1969 the agency had an American triumph to publicize: the first walk on the moon, by astronauts Neil Armstrong and Edwin Aldrin. The moon rocks they brought back were exhibited in many places worldwide and attracted avid attention. In some places, such as Kuala Lumpur, Malaysia, USIS staff arranged special viewings of the lunar samples for political and other leaders.

Relations between the United States and the Soviet Union improved in 1972 after the conclusion of a new agreement regarding exchanges in scientific, technical, and cultural affairs. This was the eighth in a series begun in 1958. The USIA took particular interest in the increasing exchanges of performing artists.

The USIA's first significant use of satellite telecasting for informing the world about U.S. government policy came when Secretary of State Kissinger delivered an important speech outlining relations with Latin America. A TV station in Caracas, Venezuela, filmed the speech with soundtracks in Spanish, Portuguese, and English and transmitted it by satellite to several countries in the region. Despite some glitches blamed on the less sophisticated techniques then in use, this effort is viewed as a milestone in TV-satellite technology. The technical achievement generated as much interest, apparently, as the substance of Kissinger's remarks.

In 1974 and 1975 the USIA had two difficult tasks: to explain the resignation of President Nixon following the Watergate scandal (in which he was implicated in covering up a burglary at the Democratic party headquarters, in the Watergate office complex), and to put the best possible face on the ending of the Vietnam War. Neither of these occasions reflected glory on the United States, but the information service preserved the dignity of the government by telling the truth.

53

Barbara Hutchison, a public affairs officer with the USIS, meets with President Gerald Ford in 1974. She had been kidnapped and held for 13 days by terrorists in Santo Domingo, Dominican Republic. Working in more than 200 posts worldwide, USIA staff can face as much danger as the armed forces.

The policy of détente was maintained during President Gerald Ford's administration, although it was sometimes strained. Anti-American feeling crystallized in attacks on USIS offices in several countries. USIA staff were threatened or attacked in Argentina, Lebanon, Iran, and Taiwan. In Santo Domingo, capital of the Dominican Republic, terrorists kidnapped USIS staffer Barbara Hutchison and held her for 13 days.

So Proudly We Hail

The celebrations to commemorate the 200th anniversary of the American Declaration of Independence provided a good opportunity for the USIA to disseminate a message more positive than news about the Watergate scandal and the Vietnam conflict had allowed. The bicentennial festivities began in May 1975 with the first showing in Paris of an exhibition entitled "The World of Franklin and Jefferson." The IBM Corporation funded the show, the noted designers Charles and Ray Eames put it together, and the USIA sponsored its showing abroad. After Paris it went to Warsaw and London, then returned for display all across the United States. Celebrations continued until the end of 1976 with a variety of spectacles, exhibits, and projects. Sailing ships from dozens of countries visited American harbors, providing an exhilarating show and inspiring scores of photographs and TV clips. USIS offices abroad showed many of these to symbolize America's pride in its past. Other countries shared the pride; Great Britain lent one of four originals of the Magna Carta (a charter from 1215 in which King John acknowledged that he was not above the law) to be exhibited in the Capitol building in Washington, D.C. France, feeling renewed pride in its 1886 gift of the Statue of Liberty, covered the bicentennial events extensively on its national television. And the USIA changed its address in Washington, D.C., from 1778 to 1776 Pennsylvania Avenue.

The Soviets too were given a share in the celebration. In Moscow, the USIA mounted an exhibit on the bicentennial called "USA—Two Hundred Years." It told the story of the two centuries of American independence by means of music, film, slides, and videotape.

Emphasizing Communication

The role of information and cultural services in the conduct of foreign affairs continued to be debated during the presidency of Jimmy Carter. The considerable overlap between the services was seen as one problem, so in 1978 responsibility for the educational and cultural activities was transferred from the Department of State to the USIA. At the same time, the agency was renamed the United States International Communication Agency (USICA). The new term acknowledged the changing role of communications technology, reflecting the belief that information is a two-way street: We have to receive as well as send messages; and we have to get a feel for public opinion in other

From left: *President Anwar Sadat of Egypt, Prime Minister Menachem Begin of Israel, and U.S. president Jimmy Carter after the signing of the Camp David accord in 1979. In a decade offering little good news, the USIA was able to acclaim this step toward peace in the Middle East as a victory for U.S. diplomacy.*

countries and relate this feedback to policy formulation. A necessary part of the communications spectrum, then, is cultural exchange. And global problems (the environment, the threat of nuclear accidents, depletion of the ozone layer, and many other issues) must also be solved through international cooperation. Agency personnel were happy to have their role clarified but were not enthusiastic about the new name. In 1982 it was changed back to USIA.

The Carter administration, in contrast to those of Kennedy and Reagan, tended to emphasize goals of mutual international understanding rather than try to achieve its own political objectives. This approach accorded with the mood of the 1970s, when Americans had tired of cold war rhetoric. Many people had begun to look with distaste upon attacks on adversaries and blatant propaganda support for U.S. policies.

President Carter scored a diplomatic triumph when he brought President Anwar Sadat of Egypt and Prime Minister Menachem Begin of Israel together at Camp David for 13 days in 1978. Media people flocked to daily press briefings while President Carter helped mediate a historic agreement by which the two nations reduced hostilities. The USICA organized and ran the press center and provided assistance for foreign journalists.

The USICA continued to bring American culture in a variety of forms to audiences all over the world. The Soviet Union got a taste of lively diplomacy when the Nitty Gritty Dirt Band, a rock group, performed there in 1977. Equally lively was the tour by the Chuck Davis Dance Company to Norway, Italy, Yugoslavia, and Greece in 1980. Less raucous was the "Rights of Man" poster show displayed at 32 USIS posts around the world in 1979.

Not everybody loved America. In 1979, during the annual Muslim pilgrimage to Mecca, in Saudi Arabia, one group of worshipers provoked a riot in which hundreds of people were killed. Iran seized the chance to accuse the United States of having instigated the incident. This obvious lie was not so obvious to Muslims in Pakistan, where demonstrators attacked and burned the American Center (run by the USIS) in Rawalpindi.

When Iranian revolutionaries seized the American embassy in Tehran, in November 1979, 4 USIS staff members were among the 52 persons held captive. The plight of the hostages cast a shadow over the remainder of Carter's administration. More bad news followed the next month when Soviet troops invaded Afghanistan, leading President Carter to announce that the United States would boycott the 1980 Summer Olympics in Moscow. A few other countries followed suit, but U.S. hopes for an international outcry never materialized. The USICA was largely alone in condemning the Soviet incursion, and even the American press questioned the wisdom of the boycott.

Reaching Out to the Third World

After Ronald Reagan was elected president in 1980, U.S. relations with the United Nations and its agencies, especially UNESCO (United Nations Educational, Scientific, and Cultural Organization), deteriorated. Some Third World countries in UNESCO are in favor of licensing journalists and imposing government controls on the press. They believe that Western news agencies are biased toward big business and against the aspirations of poor countries. This attitude was a matter of concern to the USIA; it seemed that USIS missions might be cut off from news sources and restricted in their ability to reach the public in developing countries. The United States withheld its funding and activity from UNESCO in the wake of the disagreement.

A USIS raft stops at an isolated village in Thailand. The USIA is prepared to go where radio and TV broadcasts cannot reach.

With the appointment of a new head of UNESCO in 1987, the United States agreed to resume participation in the organization. The Voice of America continued to be a mainstay of the USIA's international communications, and technological improvements in the 1980s enhanced its power. VOA's Radio Martí (the service is named for José Martí, a Cuban poet and a martyr in the fight against Spanish domination of Cuba in the 19th century) began broadcasts to Cuba in 1985 and its Televisión Martí was first beamed to Cuba in 1989. VOA broadcasts to Western Europe began again in 1985 after a 25-year lapse. In 1987 the Soviet Union stopped jamming VOA broadcasts to its territory but continued to jam broadcasts to Afghanistan. The Soviets also agreed to the establishment of a VOA bureau in Moscow with a permanent correspondent assigned to it.

The technological revolution was more spectacular in television than in radio. In January 1982 USICA broadcast worldwide in 7 languages simultaneously a 90-minute program entitled "Let Poland Be Poland." It cost an estimated $500,000 to produce and involved 345 people. The program included a wide variety of videotaped statements by world leaders as well as scenes of demonstrations and other activities indicating support for the freedom of the Polish people. The transmission required all five Intelsat satellites (modern orbiting stations for U.S. telecasts), and the producers had to translate U.S. satellite signals for foreign technical standards. Although a technical feat, the program drew criticism from some people for its cost in both money and talent. Some critics thought that the American information services should "let Poland be Poland" and not meddle in Polish affairs.

This experience and other early uses of satellite technology helped the USIA to refine both techniques and program substance. Daily television broadcasts by Worldnet to Europe began in 1985, and by 1988 the service had been expanded to serve Latin America, Africa, and the Indian Ocean region. Its extended activities are up to date—film distribution, hookups for news conferences, station assistance, and so forth.

The U.S. Advisory Commission on Public Diplomacy helped to focus the attention of the Reagan administration on opportunities to make friends abroad. The commission urged an appropriate balance between short-term and long-term objectives and between information and cultural activities. It also effectively promoted the role of the USIA in the formulation of foreign policy.

In the 1990s the USIA will be in a position to exploit any new technology its budget allows. More frequent direct satellite hookups between nations are one likely improvement.

President Ronald Reagan and Soviet premier Mikhail Gorbachev in front of the Cathedral of St. Basil, Red Square, Moscow, in May 1988. Relations between the superpowers improved in the course of four summit meetings between the two leaders, although disinformation efforts did not cease.

FIVE

Information and Disinformation in the 1980s

On the day of President Ronald Reagan's inauguration in January 1981, the American hostages in Tehran were freed—a stroke of luck for the new president, who thus gained some unearned good press. The city of New York staged a ticker tape parade to welcome back the 52 people who had been imprisoned for 444 days; in Washington, D.C., large crowds cheered them as they proceeded in a motorcade to the White House. Four USIS officers were among the hostages.

This episode had implications for U.S.-USSR relations. The Soviet Union's official stance was that the Iranian captors should have recognized the hostages' diplomatic immunity and hence freed them. But Radio Moscow, broadcasting into Iran, stood by the revolutionaries' cause and proclaimed the hostages' guilt as agents of American imperialism. President Reagan, an anticommunist by instinct, used this and other Soviet positions to justify his tough stance against the Communist bloc, and international tensions rose quickly during his tenure. He referred to the Soviet Union as the "evil empire," heightening the mutual distrust.

As part of the Reagan administration's emphasis on polishing America's image, a new term gained currency during this era: "public diplomacy." The term was coined in the 1960s as a means of distinguishing official, or government-to-government, dialogue from direct, or people-to-people, communication. Traditionally, diplomacy means explaining one government's policies to another government. Now, public diplomacy is more often the method, and its meaning is, in a loose way, what the USIA tries to do: supplement and reinforce traditional diplomacy through a mix of information, educational, and cultural activities addressed directly to the people of foreign countries. President Reagan at first was deeply suspicious of the way the Soviets conducted their public diplomacy, using distortions of the truth and other tricks to influence audiences in other countries.

Reagan was an actor by training and temperament, and some called him "the great communicator." It was only natural that he should recognize the value of communication as a diplomatic tool. The Soviets, too, placed a formidable communicator at the helm in 1985, Mikhail Gorbachev. He presented the Soviet point of view energetically and effectively in frequent and varied public statements. His book *Perestroika* (Restructuring), published in 1987, was a best-seller in much of the world. Gorbachev stressed the need for realistic communication of all kinds so that differences could be clearly understood and negotiations could proceed from a practical base. Although he is critical of certain aspects of Soviet society and politics, he chides America for seeing the Soviet Union as "evil incarnate" while viewing itself as the "embodiment of absolute good." He observes that

> American propaganda—yes, propaganda—presents America as a
> "shining city atop a hill," . . . but . . . it has millions of unfortunate
> people. . . . An almost missionary passion for preaching about human
> rights and liberties and a disregard for ensuring those same elemen-
> tary rights in their own home. . . . Endless talk about man's freedom
> and attempts to impose its way of life on others. . . . Arrogance of
> power, especially military power. . . . For what?

Gorbachev's publicity victories were supplemented by his wife Raisa. Chic and well spoken, she attracted more media attention than Nancy Reagan did during summit meetings in Washington and Moscow.

In 1981 Charles Z. Wick, the Reagan appointee for USIA director, chaired an interagency committee created to conduct "Project Truth," a campaign to refute distorted propaganda and disinformation put out by the Soviets. The

A press kit produced by the USIA for the summit meeting between U.S. president Ronald Reagan and Soviet premier Mikhail Gorbachev in December 1987. Educating the public about arms-control negotiations between NATO and the Warsaw Pact has been a significant task for the USIA in the nuclear era.

name echoed President Truman's 1950 "Campaign of Truth," which presented the American case aggressively at the height of the cold war. Under Project Truth, the USIA started publishing the newsletter *Soviet Propaganda Alert* in October 1981.

President Reagan's outspoken distrust of the Soviets mellowed somewhat after he had met Gorbachev, whose effort to remake Soviet society by means of more market-oriented policies helped to bring about a broader understanding. Generally speaking, however, the Reagan administration took a hard line toward the Soviets. For example, it never budged on Reagan's plan for space-based weapons (called "Star Wars"), justifying its own rigidity by stating that the issue brought the Soviets back to the negotiating table on arms limitations. World opinion was roundly opposed to Star Wars, and America's image sagged accordingly.

Summitry

The four summit meetings between Reagan and Gorbachev—in Geneva, Reykjavík, Washington, and Moscow—were high-water marks for the USIA as it marshaled its talents and technology to illuminate the issues in U.S.-USSR relations. In Geneva in November 1985, the VOA and Worldnet broadcast worldwide the president's address to the Soviet people, his interviews with European TV journalists, and his post-summit report to Congress. The VOA also broadcast speeches by others at the summit, in English and 41 other languages. Worldnet devoted 18 hours of satellite TV coverage to the event. The Wireless File, which electronically transmits news, background material, and policy statements, put out a steady stream of information to 204 posts, where USIS public affairs officers briefed journalists and other opinion molders. The USIA's Foreign Press Center in Washington, D.C., set up briefings for journalists from other countries. Prominent Americans in public and private life spoke to audiences in many places overseas, in person and by telephone conference call. In Geneva, 27 USIS staffers provided comprehensive support to the international media. The agency also negotiated the U.S.-Soviet cultural exchanges agreement that was signed in Geneva.

When the two leaders met again, in October 1986 at Reykjavík, Iceland, the occasion was billed only as a preliminary to some unfixed future meeting. Still,

President Reagan and Premier Gorbachev, at left, sign an arms-control treaty in the White House in December 1987. In addition to briefing the media beforehand, USIA specialists issued formal statements afterward about what the treaty entailed.

more than 1,000 delegates—and 2,000 journalists—attended. As Reykjavík boasts only 950 hotel rooms, some newspeople had to pay outrageous prices for accommodation in guesthouses and private homes. Nor was the venue for the discussions between the two leaders quite world-class: It was a modest white-shingled residence, not the customary palace or mansion.

Hopes were high in advance of the meeting that Reagan and Gorbachev would make progress on two fronts: an agreement on intermediate-range nuclear forces (INF), meaning the U.S. and Soviet missiles based in Europe; and one on testing nuclear weapons. As it turned out, the two powers came close to agreeing on deep cuts in strategic (long-range) nuclear forces and on the *elimination* of intermediate- and short-range missiles. But the result was a stalemate. Gorbachev would make no concession on Soviet missiles unless Reagan made concessions on Star Wars, which Reagan refused to do. Media coverage was heavy at Reykjavík, but the public information services were left somewhat disheartened when no major announcement resulted. The two sides even failed to agree on a date for the next summit.

The USIA began developing a public diplomacy strategy for the Washington summit nearly a year before it took place in December 1987. The staff in Washington and in the field became thoroughly familiar with all the substantive issues, particularly those relating to the INF treaty negotiations. The USIA conducted comprehensive polls of foreigners' attitudes about the U.S. and Soviet positions and analyzed the results. Thus the agency was able to advise leaders in Washington of some negative attitudes that Western Europeans held toward the United States. Because the summit negotiations concerned weapons deployed on European soil, European opinion had to be addressed. NATO allies had to be reassured that the United States remained committed to a joint defense strategy. Accordingly, the USIA developed public diplomacy programs tailored to fit each country—particularly West Germany, where the greatest number of American troops are stationed.

Taking full advantage of the USIA's technical facilities, the government explained its position to the world. President Reagan made presentations on VOA and Worldnet. Secretary of State George Shultz gave interviews at the Foreign Press Center in Washington, D.C. For the summit meeting itself, the USIA set up a combined foreign and domestic press center, which foreign journalists appreciated greatly, as it enabled them to prepare knowledgeable commentary for their readers.

The USIA's big guns saluted the conclusion of the treaty to eliminate intermediate-range nuclear forces. Thanks to the thorough preparation and involvement of policymakers in the dialogue, the signing of the INF Treaty and

President Ronald Reagan, Vice-president George Bush, and Soviet premier Mikhail Gorbachev at a summit meeting in New York in December 1988. By apprising officials in Washington about how U.S. allies and opponents react to important diplomatic events, the USIA can help American leaders to positively influence world opinion.

the instant dissemination of news about it to the world were a triumph of one kind of public diplomacy.

After the summit the USIA took part in an evaluation to identify ways to make further improvements in the public diplomacy strategy for the next summit, scheduled for spring 1988 in Moscow. The USIA advised the president that U.S. government officials should arrange to be in Moscow well in advance of the summit so that, in the week before the principals arrived, American views would have as much exposure in the foreign media as the Soviet positions. The U.S. government would analyze the objectives of the Soviets, with special attention to the points the USIA wanted to score with the people in Western countries.

In their preparations for the summit, the Soviets also paid attention to the media's role—the "summit boom," as they called it. Some Moscow streets were repaved, and some building facades were freshened or decorated. While facing the press, General Secretary Gorbachev demonstrated that he had learned a lesson from the American media: He was willing to acknowledge some disappointment with the pace of reforms under his program of perestroika, and he admitted that there were limits to his new policy of *glasnost*, translated roughly as a cross between "openness" and "publicity." This admission stood in contrast to the unwavering ideological certainty that the Kremlin had formerly presented to the world. In a presummit interview with foreign newspeople, he expressed admiration for American pragmatism, but also derided the American idea "that everything American is the best, while what others have is at least worse, if not altogether bad and unfit for use."

For political and military reasons—and probably with an eye on the media—Gorbachev began to withdraw Soviet troops from Afghanistan just two weeks before the summit. Aware that the signing of the INF Treaty at the Washington summit was a hard act to follow, he was careful not to build up expectations of significant progress on the Strategic Arms Reduction Talks (START). He said he valued the specific agreements that had been concluded, but considered more important "the regular and very productive political dialogue that we have been having."

And in fact, apart from an agreement on the verification of certain missile tests, there was not much of substance to cheer about at the summit. Staff members on both sides met to discuss matters of arms control that would be the subject of later negotiations. No breakthroughs came on trade issues or regional conflicts in Central America and southern Africa. However, the world watched and listened as President Reagan and his wife took several opportunities to remind their hosts of American views on the violation of human rights in the USSR.

Media coverage was thorough as the president and the general secretary walked together in Red Square, as Reagan visited a monastery, and as he made a speech at Moscow State University. Meanwhile, the two first ladies were interviewed while visiting a collection of icons and talking to schoolchildren. Mrs. Reagan was also photographed with the wife of Andrei Gromyko, president of the Soviet Union and former foreign minister, as they toured the Summer Palace in Leningrad and visited the grave of Soviet poet Boris Pasternak.

Was it worth the expense, time, and effort to undertake the fourth summit of the Reagan presidency when everyone recognized at the outset that the cause of arms control would not be significantly advanced? It was, if telling America's story to the world is important. The worldwide audience for this event was incalculably large. And it was worth it if the American public was thereby able to understand life in the Soviet Union a little better.

How the Other Half Lives

Preoccupation with the arms race during the first years of the Reagan administration diverted attention from educational and cultural exchanges. But people with vision in the USIA generated interest in cultural give-and-take again by managing the International Youth Exchange Initiative, which began in 1982. Under this 3-year program, students between the ages of 15 and 19 traveled for part of the year between the United States and 6 other countries: Canada, West Germany, France, Italy, Japan, and the United Kingdom. These

Cultural exchanges run by the USIA increased significantly in the 1980s. Here, an American friend signs the high school yearbook of Besma Hamada (center), an exchange student from Tunisia. Programs run by the USIA have helped Americans and foreigners learn more about each other.

68

countries constitute the Group of Seven, the largest industrial powers, whose leaders hold a summit every year.

Profiting from the improvement in the diplomatic climate, Reagan and Gorbachev signed an agreement at the Geneva summit in 1985 that provided for resumption of the educational and cultural exchanges broken off in 1979. The accord covered projects in the performing arts, exhibits, TV, films, publications, and exchange of citizens—much more than just performances in the States by the Bolshoi Ballet or in the Soviet Union by the Martha Graham Dance Company. The agreement was later extended to 1992. As part of it, the Directors' Guild of America and the Soviet State Commission of Cinematography (Goskino) agreed to exchange feature films.

Apart from the official agreement, the two leaders expressed support for the People-to-People Initiative, intended to expand direct contact between citizens of the United States and the USSR. Private sector institutions in the United States that are interested in cultural exchanges with the Soviet Union can now look to the USIA for guidance and assistance.

Antennas at the Greenville, North Carolina, relay station of the Voice of America (VOA). The VOA is the USIA's best-known operation, providing news and information to radio listeners around the world.

SIX·

Expertise and Technology

The electronic wizardry and technological miracles we live with today are often taken for granted. Many persons assume that computers, TV, and satellites will fill all our communications needs. But the USIA does not assume that. Of course, the agency employs all available media to present dynamic pictures of American life and thought, to absorb impressions of public opinion worldwide, and to interpret the changing face of international life for the global audience.

Yet the agency does not stop there, for two reasons: Some people overseas do not have access to advanced technology; and there has to be a human face connected to a voice or picture. Therefore, the USIA uses a variety of more traditional, person-to-person methods, often a combination of them. This chapter describes several of the programs through which the USIA fosters mutual understanding between Americans and people overseas.

The Voice of America

The Voice of America regularly broadcasts world news, features about American life, commentary on politics and other issues, classical and contemporary popular music, and a variety of other programs. The broadcasts go out in 44 languages, to countries in all parts of the world. To spread United States information and cultural programs, the USIA and the VOA also distribute taped and written materials to local radio stations worldwide.

The VOA is required by law to be accurate, objective, and comprehensive. It must serve as a consistently reliable and authoritative source of news, representing all of America and not just a single segment of American society. And it must offer responsible discussion and opinion on U.S. policies.

Faithful to its mandate, the VOA adheres consistently to its policy of telling it like it is, even when crime in the streets, the federal budget deficit, AIDS, or the drug problem dominate the news. A legacy of truthfulness has made the Voice of America credible in the minds of its listeners.

The VOA's credibility is probably why the Soviet Union and its allies have spent a lot of money to jam its broadcasts. In fact, the U.S. Central Intelligence Agency (CIA) has estimated that in the early 1980s, the Soviets spent $250 million a year on jamming—more than the cost of the VOA broadcasts themselves.

In 1949 jamming of VOA signals inspired the U.S. government to establish Radio Free Europe, which beamed its programs to Eastern Europe and was difficult to jam. In 1953 Radio Liberation (now called Radio Liberty) was established, its programs targeted on the Soviet Union. Radio Free Europe and Radio Liberty are operated separately from the VOA, as they are funded by the Board for International Broadcasting, an independent federal agency that also answers to Congress and the president.

Ten medium-wave and 103 shortwave transmitters, with an aggregate power of more than 26 million watts, broadcast VOA programs from the United States and 12 countries overseas. In addition, 22 commercial satellite circuits feed VOA relay stations, which in turn use medium-wave and shortwave frequencies to broadcast programs to listeners all over the world. When direct VOA broadcasts are not possible in a particular country, the USIA uses VOA transmitters to send a "correspondent's report" from Washington for reception on shortwave receivers. The program is taped and rebroadcast in a regular news slot. This technique, particularly popular in Latin America, gives the local station an impact comparable to having its own bureau in Washington, D.C.

Some improvements in technology have recently been made: Translations from English into the broadcast receiver's language are now made more rapidly with the help of the new computerized System for News and Programming (SNAP). Another aid to rapid airing of news is an electronic audio distribution system called "Sound on Demand," which can instantaneously feed on-the-scene news items to all VOA newswriters.

Radio Martí is a special service in Spanish that broadcasts to Cuba every day from 5:30 A.M. to 11:00 at night. The programs are produced in Washington and broadcast from a transmitter in Marathon, Florida. The service is meant to promote the cause of democratic freedom in Cuba. Although Fidel Castro's government tries to discourage listening, the audience is known to be large and enthusiastic. Cubans in the United States have said that many listeners appreciate the news programs (about events where the Cuban government or military has been involved, including Angola, Nicaragua, and the home island) and enjoy the music programs and special features.

Congress has allocated funds for a trial run of a television service to Cuba, TV Martí. Some critics say that the service would violate United Nations communications agreements that protect national broadcasting systems from external interference. Others say it would be easy for Cuba to block reception of its transmissions and thus render it useless. Proponents of the idea claim that it does not violate international law and that it would not be in President Fidel Castro's best interest to stifle American information and entertainment programs.

A broadcast studio for Radio Martí, the VOA operation that began transmitting to Cuba in 1987. The Cuban government has threatened to jam the broadcasts, which are critical of Cuba's Communist leadership. Jamming was a regular tactic against the VOA's operations in Eastern Europe, too, until 1987.

Another special program, VOA-Europe, presents broadcasts in English 24 hours a day to radio stations and cable systems in Western Europe. The nerve center of this far-flung operation is in Washington, D.C., where news reports are received from international monitoring services, U.S. media, and reporters based in major cities overseas. The VOA will only broadcast items that are received from two or more independent sources.

The Voice's audience is still growing. Its own quality, the spreading availability of radios in developing nations, and population increases explain the leap. In the early 1980s it reached perhaps 100 million people worldwide, 70 percent of them in Communist countries. By 1990 the estimated audience for its broadcasts—more than 1,000 hours per week, all told—was 129 million people. The titles of some of the feature programs give an idea of their diversity and potential appeal: "Science Notebook," "Agriculture Today," "Understanding Technology," and "Book World."

One way of measuring listeners' interest in the program content is to count the mail from overseas: more than 425,000 letters in 1987. Listeners write to comment on the news broadcasts and the features on sports, science, agriculture, and other topics. VOA staffers answer the letters, an exchange that seems to generate even more feedback and certainly creates goodwill. Four times a year the staff compiles a digest of audience reactions to VOA programming for the future guidance of broadcasters.

The VOA magazine, *Voice*, goes to 160,000 subscribers. Its feature articles on aspects of American culture and current events are designed to stimulate continuing interest and discussion.

The VOA gets plenty of static from competing information services, chiefly from Radio Moscow, which broadcasts 1,680 hours per week in 64 languages. The Soviets have 37 high-powered (500 kilowatt, or kw) transmitters, whereas the VOA has 6 of comparable strength, and these are teamups of old 250-kw transmitters. A large percentage of VOA transmitters date from the early 1970s. Budgetary restrictions have hampered modernization, but the service is catching up: A 500-kw shortwave transmitter began operating in West Germany in 1987, and 3 more are in the works to improve coverage of Soviet-bloc countries. In addition, a medium-wave station is being built in the Caribbean nation of Grenada, and Israel will receive a powerful relay station. Moreover, in Washington, D.C., a sophisticated master control has replaced the old-fashioned vacuum-tube system.

An indication of the success of the VOA in winning the credence and support of its audience is the fact that the Soviet Union stopped jamming its broadcasts in 1987. The halt could have stemmed from an easing of Soviet domestic

From the control room of a VOA broadcast facility, an editor lines up the daily news segment. By covering everything from science to popular music to books to local and world politics, the VOA has built an audience of about 130 million people in more than 100 countries.

controls, or it may have occurred because the jamming made potential listeners more curious—the programs took on the appeal of forbidden fruit. As of 1988, broadcasts to the USSR reached about 32 million listeners, the largest audience for any regional service.

The VOA finds itself in a tight spot sometimes when an event embarrassing to the U.S. government must be reported to the world. An example was the U-2 incident. The Voice of America could not ignore the downing, nor could it wait for the government to issue an official statement. Another unwelcome task was to report on the catastrophic error of judgment committed by the personnel of an American naval vessel when its crew shot down an Iranian passenger jet in 1988. When a Soviet fighter plane shot down a Korean passenger jet in 1983, the VOA had aired severely critical comments; now it had to deal with similar comments by others.

One offering with a large following is the program "Special English," which presents news and features in an English vocabulary of just 1,500 words. The narrators read the material slowly, for the benefit of those listeners overseas who have some grasp of English as a second language. In July 1987 the surgeon general of the United States and other experts on the AIDS crisis took part in a "Special English" program. They fielded questions by telephone from listeners in 23 countries.

Perhaps the biggest hit is "Music USA." Fans of American popular music in some countries organize clubs to listen to these broadcasts of jazz, country and western, reggae, and rock music. The programs often include comments on the lyrics and performers to help listeners understand them better.

Television, Film, Videotape

Impressions of how Americans live were first formed by the stereotypes shown in films commercially produced and distributed worldwide. Then television came to all but the poorest and most remote parts of the world, and people are learning about American life through reruns of American TV programs.

The sensational nature of commercial films and TV serials—portraying fabulously rich or wickedly corrupt characters—do not give an accurate view of American society. Nor do they treat problems of global interest in educational or productive ways. As a way to redress some of the misperceptions that TV and movies leave behind, the USIA generates its own films and TV programs. For example, the problems of illegal drug trafficking are examined in *The Trip*, a film the USIA produced in 1971. It presents the narcotics trade as a curse not only in the United States but in the drug-producing countries—especially Latin America—as well.

Since the 1960s, the growing availability of television around the world has led the USIA to use TV more than films. Now, taking advantage of satellite TV, the agency can present America's story to the global television audience through Worldnet. The USIA's department of television and film leases satellite facilities to provide links to Europe, Africa, and parts of the Middle East. In 1988 Worldnet gained access to nations around the Indian Ocean— transmitting throughout the Middle East and to most of South and East Asia. The Worldnet service is also beamed in Spanish and Portuguese to Latin

A TVRO (television receive only) dish is mounted on the roof of the U.S. embassy in Belgrade, Yugoslavia. Improved TV capacity now links USIA facilities with points in Eastern Europe.

America. In Africa antennae at four U.S. embassies receive daily Worldnet transmissions. By 1990 Worldnet will have in place all over the world a system called TVRO (Television Receive Only). The agency will install 199 of these devices, which can receive programs from European satellites.

The potential audience for Worldnet programs is about 20 million people, who can view the programs in their homes through 110 cable systems and 21 over-the-air broadcast systems. In Europe, 242 hotels carry the Worldnet programs for guests to watch in their rooms.

Worldnet also carries a mix of programs: "America Today," an overview of events in the United States and reactions to them; "Hour USA," with items on sports, music, entertainment, and business; "Scenic America"; English language instruction; and many other features. Thus Worldnet is one of America's most effective and ubiquitous ambassadors, presenting and interpreting dynamic scenes of American life and thought.

A panel of experts appears on Worldnet TV in 1987 to commemorate the opening of the National Museum of African Art in Washington, D.C. The broadcast, to six capitals in French-speaking West Africa, inaugurated satellite television service to the continent.

Besides the regularly scheduled programs, Worldnet presents "interactives," a technology that can link Washington or New York, for instance, with American diplomatic and information posts abroad. Journalists overseas can pose questions on the issues of the day to American experts and government officials. By offering an unrehearsed, uncensored exchange of views, an interactive enlivens the work and thinking of American policymakers for the benefit of foreigners.

There is more than politics to be seen and heard on interactives, however; interviews with scientists, authors, businessmen, and people who represent the entire American spectrum fill out the picture. Because the topics covered are often controversial, the programs generate comment in the local media, which redoubles the impact of the transmissions themselves.

To supplement the Worldnet service, the USIA distributes videotapes and films through its posts overseas and to foreign media and commercial outlets. One example is TV Satellite File, which offers a weekly 30-minute program of news and features to broadcasters in 110 countries. Another show, "Science World," goes out twice a week, and documentaries on videocassettes are regularly made available for foreign audiences. A sure topic for one of these documentaries would be an official visit to Washington, D.C., by a prominent foreigner.

The agency has also acquired rights to many commercial offerings. USIS libraries abroad can order videotape cassettes to lend to people who have VCRs at home. In 1987 about 8,000 tapes were borrowed, many of them from libraries in Eastern Europe. An unexpected bonus is the increase in circulation of books at the libraries that offer videotapes.

West German specialists assisted the USIA in establishing a TV station, RIAS-TV, in the American sector of Berlin. It started broadcasting in August 1988 with a news program on the U.S. presidential campaign, labor problems in Poland, and items of local interest in Berlin. With a range of 25 miles, RIAS-TV can reach 4 million viewers in East Germany and 2 million in West Berlin.

Cooperation goes both ways. The USIA helps foreign TV stations with special film coverage, cooperative projects, and other types of assistance. For example, when foreign TV producers wish to make films in America, the USIA usually provides studio facilities and helps them gain access to the people and events they want to record. The added benefit to public diplomacy of such cooperation is obvious. As the crews from two different nations come together for official purposes, they are also sharing their technical expertise; they are, in effect, improving relations and educating one another for the future.

João Mauricio Carvalho of Brazil, a fellow of the Fulbright Program, rehearses in a New York dance studio. The USIA administers the program, which offers educational and cultural exchange opportunities for people in 129 nations.

SEVEN

Outreach

Most of the USIA's programs are people-to-people projects that aim to allow for the greatest possible give-and-take between Americans and citizens of foreign countries. Some of the programs are formal educational or cultural exchanges, others are simpler and more relaxed. By bringing about exchanges of students and professionals, arranged in conjunction with the private sector, the USIA eases the strain on its limited budget and helps take the programs beyond the realm of governments.

Exchanges of students and teachers between the United States and other countries are a well-established means of enhancing understanding. The USIA oversees several, of which the Fulbright Program is the best known. When World War II was drawing to a close, Senator J. William Fulbright, who believed in beating swords into plowshares, recommended that student exchanges be financed by selling surplus U.S. war materials overseas. Later, more money came from the settlement of loans of war materials made during the war and from sales of surplus American agricultural goods. Funds obtained in these ways could not be readily converted into dollars, and therefore had to be spent in the countries where they were generated.

Dollars, however, were still needed to supplement these local currencies in order to permit two-way exchanges of American and foreign participants—for example, to meet the tuition and living costs of foreign students in the United States. At first the private sector made generous contributions, but a more comprehensive solution came with the passage of the Information and Educational Exchange Act of 1948. The act provided for direct government appropriations to support the program.

The Fulbright Program awards about 5,700 scholarships each year to Americans wishing to go abroad to study, to teach in high schools and universities, or to pursue research projects. Applicants in 120 other countries also receive awards; each year about 1,000 Fulbright scholars come from foreign countries to teach or conduct postdoctoral research in American schools and universities. The University Affiliations Program, another arm of the Fulbright system, links American colleges and universities with foreign universities by exchanging faculty in the social sciences, humanities, commu-

Wang Jian-Ye of the People's Republic of China teaching physics at Columbia University in New York on a grant from the Fulbright Program. More than 1,000 foreign scholars visit the United States each year on Fulbright grants.

Two engineers from Central America (left) at work in 1985, during the year they spent with the electric company in Minneapolis, Minnesota, as part of the Hubert H. Humphrey North-South Fellowship Program. The USIA oversees these visits.

nications, and education. The system also assists more than 3,000 graduate students who study at American universities each year. Partial scholarships from these same funds go to about 1,200 Americans with professional qualifications and about 600 graduate students below the doctoral level. A modest but important part of the program is the exchange of more than 450 elementary and secondary school teachers between the United States and other countries, mostly from Europe.

Planning and control of the Fulbright Program are fully shared by the United States and the governments of participating countries, where local institutions have administrative responsibility. The selection of foreign grant recipients is made by a joint committee of public officials and private citizens, both natives of the participating country and Americans living there. Similarly, host-country officials must approve Americans chosen for visits abroad. This sharing of responsibility makes the program especially acceptable abroad.

The program does not try to score public relations points in the short term, and it does not consider the scholars' political stands. Participants on both sides are selected on the basis of academic and professional merit. In the United

83

States, the government does not even have a say in selecting and supervising the American participants; this duty is entrusted to the Board of Foreign Scholarships, a 12-member group of private citizens appointed by the U.S. president and drawn largely from university faculties.

In addition to these exchanges, the Fulbright Program administers the Hubert H. Humphrey North-South Fellowship Program, which provides a year of specially tailored study at the graduate level in the United States for professional people from Third World countries. The recipients of these fellowships also gain practical experience in work related to their professions.

In 1985 a new program was initiated, targeted at undergraduate students from poor Central American countries. They study English intensively and then attend American colleges and universities. By 1988 the program had benefited 238 students.

Backing up these scholarship and exchange programs, the USIA's 345 offices around the world provide advice to people who wish to study in the United States. The agency also works with American colleges, universities,

Since the 1950s, American cultural figures have gone abroad on tours arranged by the USIS. Poet Carl Sandburg is shown here in 1960 before TV cameras in Stockholm, Sweden, the land of his ancestors.

and communities on programs to help foreign students in the United States, who in 1988 numbered about 344,000.

Fulbright exchanges have been opening the mind and enriching the experience of thousands of participants for more than 40 years. Past American participants—including economist Paul Samuelson, writer John Updike, actor Stacy Keach, Senator Daniel P. Moynihan, and soprano Anna Moffo—have returned home to make valuable contributions to U.S. society. Many foreigners who studied in America have also risen to prominent positions in their governments: a former Swedish prime minister, a Belgian defense minister, an Indonesian foreign affairs minister, and a Colombian finance minister.

International Visitor Program

On the invitation of American embassies, some 3,000 prominent people from foreign countries visit the United States each year. They are political leaders, media personalities, educators, or persons who are well known in the business world or in various professions. Upwards of 2,400 other foreign political and professional figures visit under sponsorship by their governments or at their own expense. Visits under this program are coordinated by local organizations and assisted by volunteers all over America.

International Youth Exchange

The International Youth Exchange Initiative is a program for people between the ages of 15 and 25 who want to live, study, and work in another country. The USIA provides grants to private organizations that arrange for foreign teenagers and young adults to come to the United States, and for their American counterparts to go to foreign countries for a year of broadening experience—staying in an ordinary home, going to school, working on group projects, and so forth. Although these exchanges have been going on for a number of years, the program received new impetus in 1982 when President Reagan announced the expansion of exchanges between the United States and six other countries. More than 22,000 young people received grants for exchange travel, work, and study in the 3 years of this program.

Artistic Ambassador Program

Music, perhaps the most international language, is the medium of communication for those who take part in the Artistic Ambassador Program. They are pianists, violinists, cellists, and others—aspiring artists who have not yet had a musical performing career. Nominated by music schools and conservatories, they then audition before a panel of well-known musicians. Those chosen go on overseas tours for four to eight weeks. They give concerts and conduct musical workshops and lecture-recitals at conservatories and music schools. The program began in 1983, and by the end of 1988, 28 musicians had reached appreciative audiences in 63 countries. By premiering new works by U.S. composers, commissioned by the government for this program, these musical ambassadors have given audiences and music students abroad a deeper appreciation of American music and music training.

Libraries and Books

Every year 4 million people in 96 countries avail themselves of the facilities of United States Information Service libraries and reading rooms—159 of them, plus 111 binational centers in 24 countries. All together, there are close to 950,000 books and 21,000 periodicals in these libraries, many of them selected with a view to helping readers learn about the United States. American publishers donated about 500,000 books in 1985, mainly for distribution in Third World countries.

The Soviet Union outstrips the United States in the book race, translating and distributing books at subsidized prices in underdeveloped countries to promote Soviet political ideas and culture. Recognizing this fact, the USIA has increased the allocation of resources to library programs. The agency provides technical assistance at home and abroad in the publication of textbooks, popular and literary books, condensations (abridged editions), and serializations (excerpts that run in magazines). An average of 600,000 copies of such publications, in English and 25 other languages, are distributed abroad each year. To popularize American books overseas, the USIA also stages international book fairs and campaigns.

Cultural Centers

There are 200 USIS cultural centers around the world in nearly 100 countries, many of them binational. Each year some 400,000 people attend English language classes at these centers.

The East-West Center in Honolulu holds a special place in the program, bringing together 2,000 people annually to consider issues that concern Americans and Asians, from commerce to the environment. Participants from 60 countries come from universities, government institutions, the media, and other professions. The USIA provides 80 percent of the funding for the center, which is now seeking a greater proportion of its support from the private sector.

The library of the USIS building in Lagos, Nigeria. Many of the books in USIS libraries are chosen to help people abroad better understand life in the United States; U.S. publishers donate some of the books, especially to Third World nations.

English Teaching

Every year almost 400,000 people take lessons in English at facilities assisted by the USIA. The courses used to be taught mainly by American teachers, but now English language specialists train locally recruited teachers and help produce instructional materials. Specialists in the teaching of English as a foreign language (TOEFL) stationed in Washington assist USIS offices with their programs. They also provide supplementary materials for teachers and trainees. The agency's quarterly journal, *English Teaching Forum*, has more than 100,000 readers each year. To reinforce these programs, the USIA contracted with a publishing company to produce teaching packages for beginning and intermediate levels. It uses video and audio cassettes, textbooks, workbooks, readings, and instructors' aids for work in and out of the classroom.

Elham Mohammad, video librarian in the USIS center in San'a, Yemen. She is an advanced student in the English language program there, where 400 students can use videocassettes as well as books to aid their studies.

The Press

Another element of the USIA's outreach is the press, which is served abroad by a number of facilities. The most extensive, called the Wireless File, is a radio teletype network and a computer linkup between the United States and USIA posts abroad. Five times each week U.S. headquarters transmits policy statements and commentary in English, Spanish, French, and Arabic to five regional centers. These centers distribute the material to more than 150 branch posts and information offices in American embassies to be used as background material and to send to overseas news outlets. The USIS officers include the material in their press releases, thereby providing reliable information for the government and the media in many countries.

The Express File, a service started in October 1987, supplements the Wireless File by making news items directly available to media organizations everywhere. And USIA posts overseas receive printed materials on American life and thought—features, reprints of magazine articles, photographs, and so forth—that are also made available to local press outlets. The news feature service called "Dateline America" is an example.

Another press service is the *Soviet Propaganda Alert*, available to USIA posts overseas. Its purpose is to expose any disinformation efforts made by anti-American governments, usually Communist nations allied with the USSR. When news breaks that could be used as propaganda, U.S. information officers turn to a cabled fast-guidance service that gives them quick access to officials in Washington, D.C.

Foreign Press Centers

The USIA helps foreign correspondents and journalists, both those working full-time in the United States and those visiting on short assignments, through centers in Washington, New York, and Los Angeles. These centers help foreign reporters obtain press credentials and make contact with the people who make the news.

Publications

The USIA puts out 14 magazines in 16 languages. They contain reprints or translations of articles published in American periodicals, as well as material produced expressly for a particular readership. Some of these periodicals are translated into local languages at USIA posts in the field. Some examples are: *America Illustrated*, a monthly magazine published in Russian and distributed in the USSR; *Topic*, a bimonthly published in French and English for sub-Saharan Africa; *Economic Impact*, a quarterly in English and Spanish; *Problems of Communism*, an English-language bimonthly; *Al Majal*, a monthly magazine in Arabic distributed in North Africa and the Middle East; *Dialogue*, a quarterly targeted at intellectual readers and published in seven languages; *Trends*, published in Japan; and *Span*, published in India.

Local staff members promote the magazine Span, *published by the USIS for readers in India. The agency publishes 14 different magazines in 16 languages, including translations of articles from U.S. periodicals as well as material aimed specifically at the local population.*

Exhibitions

All the devices of show biz come together when the USIA stages one of its traveling exhibitions, but they are not staged productions. The point is to show the world various aspects of life in America—agriculture, telecommunications, theater, education, sports, and many other themes. Private companies and individuals sometimes lend or donate products for the displays and provide guides to the exhibits or other kinds of support. If the exhibition's theme is the computer revolution, for example, it is logical for Apple, AT&T, and Hewlett-Packard to donate their wares—as in fact they did for the Tsukuba Expo (1985) in Japan. The expos have other informational offerings, too—lectures, shows, seminars, and receptions focused on the theme. American guides demonstrate equipment, explain displays, and answer questions, allowing the audience to enter into the show and discuss it with them.

There are 16 or 18 major exhibits every year, shown in one place for a month before leaving for another city or town, and as many as 2.5 million people visit these displays. Some of the exhibitions are held in places where the people have had little or no contact with American people and customs, such as provincial towns and cities in Eastern-bloc countries. One particularly successful exhibit in 1988 (part of the implementation of a cultural accord with the Soviet Union signed three years before) displayed some conveniences common in America, such as frozen dinners and photocopiers. The show's seventh stop, at the industrial city of Magnitogorsk, in the shadow of the Ural Mountains, attracted some 8,000 visitors every day. The visitors had previously heard and read mainly about drugs, street crime, and unemployment in America; now they got a glimpse of some of the more attractive features of life in the United States, as well as the chance to ask questions of the Russian-speaking Americans who accompanied the show.

For every world's fair or exposition, the USIA is responsible for erecting the U.S. pavilion. Some of the fairs feature a specific theme, such as transportation or communications. Others are more universal, such as "Man and His World." The U.S. pavilion at these events always attracts large crowds. The theme of the U.S. exhibit at the Tsukuba Expo was computers and artificial intelligence. At the Vancouver Expo, in 1986, the topic was the space shuttle program, and at the 1987 World Expo in Brisbane, Australia, the U.S. exhibit was called "Sports and Its Science." In 1992, the 500th anniversary of Columbus's first voyage to the New World, the U.S. pavilion at the World's Fair in Seville, Spain, will celebrate "The Age of Discovery."

On a somewhat smaller scale are the trade fairs that the USIA mounts to reinforce and extend commercial displays presented by American companies. Recent trade fairs have featured food production and marketing, communications technology, the space station program, and entrepreneurship. Still more modest are the poster displays, called paper shows, that the USIA produces, prints, and distributes to U.S. embassies and cultural centers overseas. A cluster of curious people usually studies these displays, which are often shown in glass cases on or near the street. Sometimes they are set up in schools or in meeting rooms. The themes, again, are varied—everything from children's books to the Statue of Liberty.

Performing and Fine Arts

Arts America is the name of the program through which the USIA sends performers and fine art exhibitions overseas. When an American embassy requests a particular kind of tour, the USIA asks for recommendations from the

Visitors to the 1987 Information USA exhibit in Moscow watch a video of Cindy Lauper singing "Girls Just Want to Have Fun." USIS shows promoting technological advances have drawn enormous crowds in the Soviet Union and elsewhere.

National Endowment for the Arts and/or the National Endowment for the Humanities on the types of artists or exhibits that would be desirable and available. On the basis of these recommendations, the Arts America staff decides on the appropriate package. The performers and exhibits usually go to countries selected because they have not had much exposure to American culture. The artists also often conduct workshops and seminars to deepen mutual understanding.

Arts America has a limited budget and cannot afford to mount very many tours or exhibits by itself. Nor does it subsidize individuals or groups seeking funding for their tours. Often, however, it will cosponsor tours planned by private groups or help these groups in any way it can. Every year Arts America sends all U.S. embassies a list of artists who have been endorsed by the National Endowment for the Arts and are available for privately arranged tours. Its funds may be used to cover international travel, living expenses, performance fees, and staging costs (in the case of the performing arts), or shipping costs, insurance, and publication of catalogs in appropriate languages (in the case of fine art exhibitions). The USIA can also arrange to share costs with a foreign cosponsor. Sometimes, too, Arts America offers to cosponsor or extend a commercially funded tour. The program also organizes U.S. participation in major international exhibitions, such as the Venice Biennale, and international arts festivals, such as the Edinburgh Festival.

Speakers

In the American Participant Program (AmPart), prominent Americans are invited to undertake short speaking tours abroad. The AmParts are experts in economics, science, social problems, literature, arts, politics, or other fields of interest to people in the countries they visit. Depending on the speaker's field of expertise and the wishes of his foreign hosts, the AmPart may deliver an informal lecture followed by discussion with a small group of experts in his field, or a more formal talk with time for questions from a larger audience. He or she

As part of the Arts America program, Milton Batiste led his octet, the Dejan's Olympia Brass Band, to Managua, Nicaragua, in 1988. The public's response was tremendous, pointing out the value of nonpolitical diplomacy through the arts.

may be interviewed by the press, make official calls on government officials, or meet with intellectuals, labor leaders, students, artists—in short, people from all walks of life.

Each year about 800 American experts participate in this program. Some of the distinguished persons who have been AmParts at some time in their careers are Warren Burger, former chief justice of the Supreme Court; Betty Friedan, noted author and feminist; Max Kampelman, U.S. negotiator at the Geneva arms reduction talks; and Jeane Kirkpatrick, former ambassador to the United Nations. If, as sometimes happens, a sought-after authority on some aspect of American life is unable to travel abroad as an AmPart, the USIA can bring speakers and audiences abroad together by electronic means.

Sports America

This program sends well-known American sports specialists overseas on short assignments to give lectures, conduct workshops, and make public appearances, or, for a somewhat longer period, to run training camps for athletes. Lee Evans, who set a world record in the 400-meter race in 1968, has participated in this program. American boxers, among them George Foreman, Floyd Patterson, Archie Moore, and Muhammad Ali, have worked with athletes overseas under the sponsorship of Sports America. Malvin Whitfield, the Olympic gold-medal winner in the 800-meter event in 1948 and 1952, has operated training camps in Africa. In 1988, before the Olympics in Seoul, he ran boxing and track-and-field camps in Zimbabwe and Malawi, along with other prominent coaches who held clinics and instructed athletes from 13 African countries.

Cultural Property

Every year, international art dealers strike many shady deals involving cultural artifacts stolen from various nations. One such deal that came under public scrutiny occurred in 1988, when The Getty Museum in California bought a statue of the Greek goddess of love, Aphrodite, dating from the 5th century B.C. and valued at $20 million. The statue had probably been excavated illegally in Sicily. Most such deals do not attract media attention, but stealing art treasures is big business: An estimated $1 billion worth of art and artifacts is smuggled out of their countries of origin each year to be sold on the international market. The heritage of many cultures, particularly in the Third World, is threatened by unscrupulous dealing in archaeological and ethnological artifacts. Concern over this menace to the world's cultures has impelled the

The Sports America program supported Muhammad Ali on his private visit to Islamabad, Pakistan, in 1987. The former heavyweight boxing champion spoke from a podium rigged up like a boxing ring, an idea of the USIS staff.

United States to take part in an international effort to prevent smuggling of national art treasures. Under the Cultural Property Act of 1968, the USIA coordinates the efforts of the U.S. government with international organizations such as Interpol, an international police agency, in assisting countries that ask for help in protecting their cultural heritage. A committee of archaeologists, art dealers, museum officials, and private citizens advises the agency in these matters.

The point of all this cultural exchange is to underscore the message that as a means of international cooperation, public diplomacy is an extension of formal diplomacy. People, paintings, electronics, sports gear, and books can penetrate ideological barriers even when geopolitical conflicts mar the world scene. The USIA's outreach programs are meant to put America's best foot forward.

The theme of this Information USA exhibit, put on by the USIS in the Soviet Union, is Electronics in Stores. Increased cooperation with private industry has helped the agency publicize the American way of life.

EIGHT

Still Carrying
the Torch

The USIA was no infant when it came into being. It was more like the goddess Athena springing fully grown and fully armed from the head of Zeus, ready to do battle. The head of Zeus in this analogy is the Department of State. Already in 1953, when the USIA, Athena in this analogy, was established, it was an experienced and effective conduit of information, operating as an independent unit in the State Department.

Since then, the USIA has flourished as an independent bureau. Between 1953 and 1988 its budget increased from less than $100 million to more than $800 million. Its physical facilities in Washington, D.C., and overseas have expanded greatly. Its staffers are now professional and sophisticated in both political science and communications technology. In one way, however, they are still like the people with whom they work abroad: They speak the local language.

The technological miracles that have been wrought in communications sciences explain much of the USIA's growth. TV was in its infancy in 1953. Radio was at an early stage of development. Satellites and computers were only on the drawing board. Today the USIA is in instant touch with news bureaus and can capture the attention of audiences anywhere in the world by any medium it chooses.

Technicians from the African nation of Liberia visit a Voice of America control room in Washington, D.C. By organizing cultural, educational, and scientific exchange programs and by broadcasting worldwide over the VOA and other systems, the USIA keeps America's international ties strong.

The agency's place as a highly regarded instrument of government is now accepted. It has a hand in administering foreign policy by working with the Department of State and other agencies of the government. Its information techniques and educational and cultural programs, once separated, now reinforce one another as they influence hearts and minds worldwide. Whether the vehicle is a broad statement of national policy or a performance by a rock singer, America's message is brought home to the audience in Moscow and Maputo.

If technology has allowed for the USIA's expansion, shifts in the East-West conflict—from cold war and crisis to détente and peaceful coexistence—have required it. USIA information and exchange programs have engendered a climate of rapprochement with the nations whose differing ideologies once seemed so alien. As recently as the early 1970s, most people would not have considered possible today's level of cooperation between the superpowers.

Relations with the United Nations and Third World countries have not always been easy, either. Still, the USIA has helped the United States maintain a positive image despite charges of neocolonialism and militarism. Exchanges of students and cultural events help offset some foreign hostility toward American capitalism. At the same time that they denounce American big business and American support of the racist apartheid regime in South Africa, people in other countries eagerly seek the goods of the American way of life—rock music, blue jeans, Hollywood films, and technological expertise. Leaders in Marxist countries, recognizing that they cannot ignore public opinion, are making social and economic concessions. The Solidarity movement in Poland is one example of the force that exposure to free-world values can exert on government policies.

The USIA now has the organization, the people, and the technology to project the positive side of American society in ever more creative and convincing ways; and it can deal with the negative elements, whatever they may be, in truthful and constructive ways.

Tonight's newscast and tomorrow morning's paper give us a mixture of distress and hope—distress over the persistence of hunger and war in many parts of the world, and hope that scientific advances and increased international understanding will gradually overcome these evils.

U.S. Information Agency

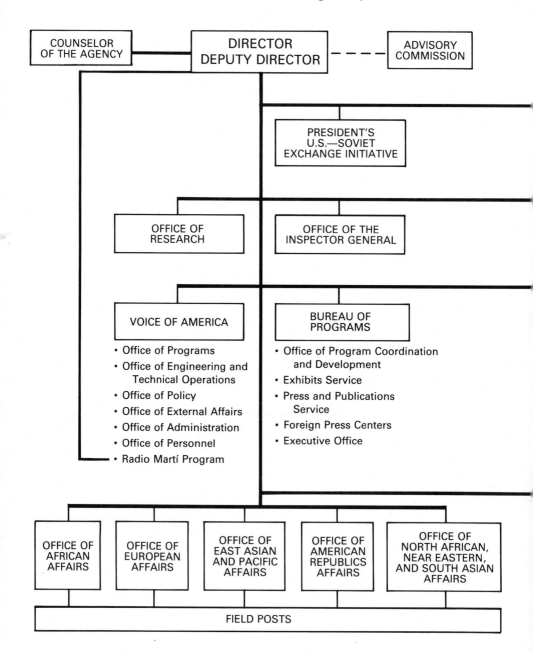

COUNSELOR OF THE AGENCY

DIRECTOR
DEPUTY DIRECTOR

ADVISORY COMMISSION

PRESIDENT'S
U.S.—SOVIET
EXCHANGE INITIATIVE

OFFICE OF
RESEARCH

OFFICE OF THE
INSPECTOR GENERAL

VOICE OF AMERICA

- Office of Programs
- Office of Engineering and Technical Operations
- Office of Policy
- Office of External Affairs
- Office of Administration
- Office of Personnel
- Radio Martí Program

BUREAU OF PROGRAMS

- Office of Program Coordination and Development
- Exhibits Service
- Press and Publications Service
- Foreign Press Centers
- Executive Office

OFFICE OF AFRICAN AFFAIRS

OFFICE OF EUROPEAN AFFAIRS

OFFICE OF EAST ASIAN AND PACIFIC AFFAIRS

OFFICE OF AMERICAN REPUBLICS AFFAIRS

OFFICE OF NORTH AFRICAN, NEAR EASTERN, AND SOUTH ASIAN AFFAIRS

FIELD POSTS

100

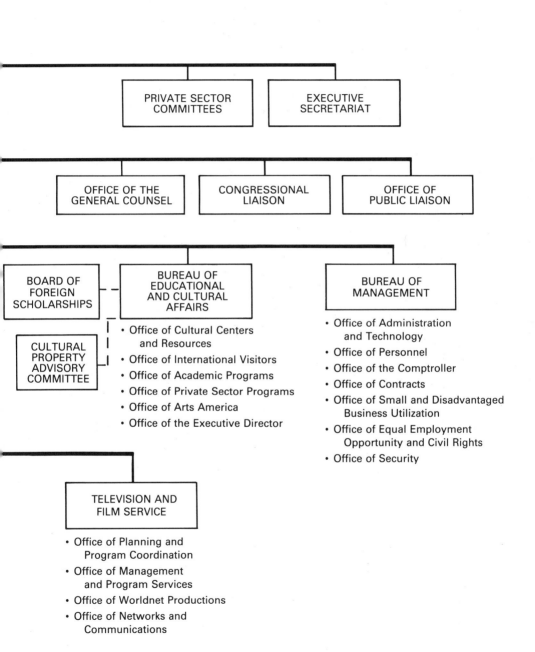

PRIVATE SECTOR COMMITTEES

EXECUTIVE SECRETARIAT

OFFICE OF THE GENERAL COUNSEL

CONGRESSIONAL LIAISON

OFFICE OF PUBLIC LIAISON

BOARD OF FOREIGN SCHOLARSHIPS

BUREAU OF EDUCATIONAL AND CULTURAL AFFAIRS

BUREAU OF MANAGEMENT

CULTURAL PROPERTY ADVISORY COMMITTEE

- Office of Cultural Centers and Resources
- Office of International Visitors
- Office of Academic Programs
- Office of Private Sector Programs
- Office of Arts America
- Office of the Executive Director

- Office of Administration and Technology
- Office of Personnel
- Office of the Comptroller
- Office of Contracts
- Office of Small and Disadvantaged Business Utilization
- Office of Equal Employment Opportunity and Civil Rights
- Office of Security

TELEVISION AND FILM SERVICE

- Office of Planning and Program Coordination
- Office of Management and Program Services
- Office of Worldnet Productions
- Office of Networks and Communications

GLOSSARY

Cold war   A conflict over ideological differences (such as that between the United States and the Soviet Union) conducted not with arms but with power politics, economic pressure, espionage, hostile propaganda, and, often, exclusion of the opponent's citizens.

Containment   The policy or process of preventing the expansion of a hostile ideology.

Détente   A relaxation of strained relations and political tensions between nations.

Diplomacy   The art and practice of conducting negotiations between nations; skill in handling affairs without arousing hostility.

Disinformation   False information deliberately and often covertly spread (as by the planting of rumors) in order to influence public opinion or obscure the truth.

Glasnost   A basic policy of Soviet leader Mikhail Gorbachev. The word translates as a combination of "publicity" and "openness"; the policy encourages free expression about public affairs in every sphere of Soviet life, without fear of reprisal. The aim is to identify and correct shortcomings in the political system.

Hegemony   The dominant influence or authority of one nation over others.

Imperialism   The extension of a nation's power by means of territorial acquisition or political and economic influence.

Independent agency   A federal agency that is not part of the cabinet-level executive departments but is often organized like these departments and headed by persons who report to the president. An independent agency performs service rather than regulatory functions.

Iron curtain   A political, military, and ideological barrier (such as the one cutting off Soviet-controlled Eastern Europe from Western Europe) that prevents free communication, travel, and economic relations between two geographic areas.

Isolationism   The theory and practice of noninvolvement in the affairs of other nations.

Perestroika   A basic policy of Soviet leader Mikhail Gorbachev, roughly translated as "restructuring"; intended to shift the Soviet people's ideas about domestic and foreign policy away from centralized planning and toward individual responsibility, open discussion, and personal involvement in the nation's economic and political life.

Propaganda   Ideas, information, or rumors spread by deliberate effort through any medium of communication in order to further one's cause or damage an opposing cause.

Public diplomacy   A supplement and reinforcement to traditional diplomacy, which explains and advocates U.S. policies through a mix of information and educational and cultural activities addressed directly to the people rather than to the governments of foreign countries.

Radio Martí   USIA-sponsored radio broadcasts in Spanish to Cuba, begun in 1985 to counteract the policies of the Castro regime and named for the 19th-century Cuban poet and martyr José Martí.

Rapprochement   The establishment or restoration of harmony and friendly relations.

Voice of America   A variety of USIA-sponsored news reports, features, music, and commentary programs, broadcast in 44 languages to all parts of the world and designed to present an objective, informative, and comprehensive view of life in the United States.

SELECTED REFERENCES

Board of Foreign Scholarships. *Forty Years: The Fulbright Program 1946–1986.* Washington, DC: Twenty-third Annual Report of the Board of Foreign Scholarships, 1986.

Bogart, Leo. *Premises for Propaganda: The United States Information Agency's Operating Assumptions in the Cold War.* New York: The Free Press, 1976.

"Can the News Abroad Come Home?" *New York Times,* November 25, 1987.

Fulbright and Other Grants for Graduate Study Abroad, 1989–1990. New York: Institute for International Education, 1988.

Gorbachev, Mikhail. *Perestroika: New Thinking for Our Country and the World.* New York: Harper & Row, 1988.

Hansen, Allen C. *USIA: Public Diplomacy in the Computer Age.* New York: Praeger Publishers, 1984.

Henderson, John W. *The United States Information Agency.* New York: Praeger Publishers, 1969.

Malone, Gifford D. *Organizing the Nation's Public Diplomacy.* Vol. 11 in Exxon Education Foundation Series on Rhetoric and Political Discourse, Political Advocacy and Cultural Communication. Lanham, MD: University Press of America, 1988.

"Reagan's 'Moscow Spring.'" *Newsweek,* June 13, 1988, 16–22.

United States Advisory Commission on Public Diplomacy. *1986 Report.* Washington, DC: U.S. Advisory Commission on Public Diplomacy, 1986.

United States Advisory Commission on Public Diplomacy. *Public Diplomacy: Lessons from the Washington Summit.* Washington, DC: A Report of the U.S. Advisory Commission on Public Diplomacy, 1988.

United States Information Agency. *Disinformation: Soviet Active Measures and Disinformation Forecast.* (A monthly newsletter.) Washington, DC: USIA, 1988.

United States Information Agency. *USIA Update.* (A monthly newsletter.) Washington, DC: USIA, 1988.

Voice of America. *Voice of America 1988: Organization and Operations.* Washington, DC: VOA, 1988.

INDEX

Clinton L. and Lois T. Doggett are graduates of Oberlin College. From 1946 to 1973 Mr. Doggett, who also received an M.A. in economics from Johns Hopkins University, worked in U.S. foreign aid missions in Europe, Asia, and Africa, and Mrs. Doggett taught English literature and other subjects in international schools. Since 1974 the authors have been working together on economic development projects with the ministries of African countries.

Arthur M. Schlesinger, jr., served in the White House as special assistant to Presidents Kennedy and Johnson. He is the author of numerous acclaimed works in American history and has twice been awarded the Pulitzer Prize. He taught history at Harvard College for many years and is currently Albert Schweitzer Professor of the Humanities at the City College of New York.

PICTURE CREDITS